THE
BACKPACKER'S
HANDBOOK

THE
BACKPACKER'S
HANDBOOK

HUGH McMANNERS

DORLING KINDERSLEY
LONDON • NEW YORK • STUTTGART

A Dorling Kindersley Book

Project Editor
Francis Ritter
Designer
Colette Ho
Managing Editor
Krystyna Mayer
Managing Art Editor
Derek Coombes
DTP Designer
Cressida Joyce
Production Manager
Maryann Rogers

US Editor
Jill Hamilton
US Consultant
Paul G. Marcolini, EMT-P
Director, Wilderness Medical Associates

First American Edition, 1995
2 4 6 8 10 9 7 5 3 1

Published in the United States by
Dorling Kindersley Publishing, Inc.,
95 Madison Avenue,
New York, New York 10016

Copyright © 1995
Dorling Kindersley Limited, London

Library of Congress
Cataloging-in-Publication Data

McManners, Hugh.
The backpacker's handbook / by Hugh
McManners. — 1st American ed. p . cm .
Includes index.
ISBN 1-56458-852-1
1. Backpacking--Handbooks, manuals, etc.
I. Title.
GV199.6.M43   1995
796.5' 1--dc20
94-32042
CIP

Reproduced by GRB, Italy
Printed and bound in Italy by Graphicom

CONTENTS

1
Getting Started

2
Equipment and Techniques

3
Moving on the Trail

5
Dealing with Emergencies

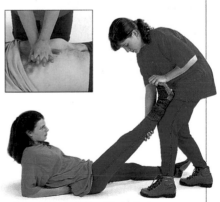

4
Camping in the Wild

INTRODUCTION

The great advantage of a well-designed backpack over other forms of luggage is freedom of movement. With everything you require hoisted comfortably onto your back, you have no need to tie yourself down to a fixed base. Whether you are walking through a national park, climbing a mountain, photographing wildlife, or traveling around the world from country to country, you are self-sufficient and can respond without hindrance to any adventure that may come your way.

In the Jungle
A trek into the jungle can take you far from the nearest road.

Expanding Your Horizons

Reducing your equipment to a light, minimal load brings many exciting activities within your reach. Touring vacations on a bicycle or in any kind of boat, example, become a real possibility when you restrict yourself to a backpack. Furthermore, knowing that you can carry all your equipment yourself in an emergency makes it possible to go far off the beaten track, and to walk out again unaided if you meet with a setback. Backpackers, including those with special interests, such as fishing, rock climbing, caving, and even bird watching, can find remote sites that less adventurous individuals could never hope to see.

The Right Equipment

Buying equipment for backpacking is expensive and confusing, even for experts. Constant technological advances produce camping equipment that is ever more lightweight, warm, comfortable, and quick-drying. Be on your guard, however, against spending money on items that you may never use and which, although lightweight, collectively weigh down your pack. Many such objects are marketed as

On a Bicycle
If you are using good roads, panniers take the weight off your back.

backpackers' versions of household items, with the suggestion that you can be as comfortable on the trail as at home. This book shows how being prepared to improvise in the wild contributes infinitely more to your comfort than carrying a large collection of gadgets on your back.

In the Mountains
A backpack containing all your vital equipment is indispensable for safe mountaineering.

Becoming a Backpacker

Regardless of whether you intend something seriously and ruggedly adventurous, or simply some low-budget sight-seeing, you must plan an itinerary and determine what you need. Carrying your load must be well within your physical capacity, and important items should be easily accessible. Every traveler also needs to know how to seek shelter, obtain water and food, navigate with compass and map, and be able to cross rough terrain in all climates. You might not intend to walk across a desert or through a jungle, but you never know when you might have to, or when extreme weather might change the local conditions and force a rapid departure.

On Skis
Backpacks enable you to set up camp even in frozen conditions.

Emergency Action

Backpacking is always an adventurous choice, and all true adventure includes some element of risk. This book provides advice for a variety of dangerous situations, with first-aid guidelines for health problems that you could experience on the trail.

Visiting Monuments
Some ancient buildings are inaccessible to everyone except the intrepid backpacker.

Going Your Own Way

Backpackers share an independence of spirit and a readiness to apply common sense to any problem they encounter. You can be happier in the wild than at home – if you learn how to do things differently.

1
GETTING
STARTED

TIME SPENT CAREFULLY PLANNING a backpacking trip is never wasted. Plan early, long before you set your departure date, determining what you want to do and examining every option. You may need to enroll in a first-aid course, plan a fitness regimen, have your vaccinations, organize your finances, choose companions, and buy equipment. If traveling with a tour company, check its safety record and make sure that you would not save money by organizing the trip yourself.

FIRST CONSIDERATIONS

THE KEY TO SUCCESSFUL PLANNING is to get started as early as possible. Working backward from the date on which you wish your trip to start, make a calendar of dates by which various arrangements must be completed. Allow plenty of time for the processing of official items such as passports and visas.

Entry Documents

Some destinations will not require you to have a visa or even a passport. Others are strict and take a long time to process visa applications. You may be required to supply references, a certain number of photographs of a specific size, a copy of your birth certificate, immunization record, financial or professional declarations, and a return air ticket, so discover what you will need before you apply and try to find out how long the process will take. Some countries require that you apply in person at their embassy. Generally, it is best to secure all your visas before you depart from your home country.

Airline Tickets

Air fares include standard tickets of various classes (first, business, and coach), apex tickets (which must be booked in advance and are not usually adaptable if your plans change), and charter fares. In addition, there are round-the-world tickets, allowing stop-offs at various locations. Charter fares can be bought inexpensively, but your flight may be crowded, delayed, or scheduled to land at an inconvenient hour. If you are taking heavy equipment, buying a ticket with a generous baggage allowance may save you money.

Foreign Currency

Due to black market trade in foreign currency, some governments demand that you exchange it through official channels and have documentation to prove it. Similarly, foreign goods can command high prices and you may have to prove when you leave that you have not sold any item. Take copies of a typed list, signed by your own customs, of everything you carry, with serial numbers, dates, places of purchase, and prices. The document will help in dealing with any foreign customs query, as well as theft or insurance claims.

Medical Precautions

The immunizations you need vary according to your destination *(see page 17)*; series of injections can take several weeks. You should also allow time for dental checkups and have any dental repairs done before you go. Do not neglect to arrange medical insurance, because treatment abroad can be very expensive, and you could need a medical evacuation home should you develop a serious health problem. Although vacation insurance can be bought quickly, medical insurance may take time and require a checkup.

Fitness Training

Everybody benefits from exercise and fitness training, and a backpacking vacation offers an excellent reason to make a start *(see page 18)*. It is unwise to go straight from a sedentary job to carrying a heavy pack across rough terrain; you must first get fit, then get used to walking distances in boots, carrying weight. Working up to fitness must be gradual, over at least three months. If you try to achieve too much too soon, you can easily injure yourself and spoil your trip. Training also highlights your physical limitations, making you less likely to overreach yourself in rugged country.

Outdoor Clothing

Your choice of clothing and footwear is determined largely by the climate and terrain in which you will be operating. Talking to people with experience of the region is invaluable. You can buy your inner layers of clothing *(see page 32)* at a reasonable price at any reputable clothing store. Good weatherproof items, such as boots, slickers, and insulating garments, tough, lightweight jungle wear, or protective, heat-retaining clothing for nights in the desert, are costly and are best bought at specialized retailers. Buy your boots several months before traveling and break them in before your departure.

Navigation Aids

Maps of distant places can be difficult to find, so start your search early. Some countries restrict distribution of their maps for security reasons, while others have only outdated maps. Buy any good map you find because maps may be unavailable on the spot. Obtain a good Silva-type compass *(see page 90)* and practice navigation near your home. Getting lost in safe country can teach you many valuable lessons. After practicing navigation, you could buy a prismatic compass *(see page 91)* if you intend to get far away from roads.

Camping Gear

Before spending money, borrow camping items for trial on weekend trips, buying only when you know exactly what you need. In the shops, find out about the full range of equipment, not just the things you might purchase. Listen to what the sales staff say but do not be persuaded against your better judgment to add to the weight of your pack. High-quality items on your list will be more affordable in the end-of-season sales. Remember that stove fuel is banned from flights, so buy a stove for which you know fuel will be obtainable on arrival.

Traveling Companions

Ideally, the individuals in a backpacking group should have complimentary skills. Introductory expeditions pinpoint individual preferences and weaknesses, help the team to gel, and enable members to share their expertise in first aid, climbing, equipment, photography, and other areas. It is unwise to go on the trail with people who are complete strangers and might prove unreliable in a crisis, or make you feel isolated and lonely. Even friends can behave in unpredictable ways on the trail. If you do join an unknown group, make every effort to talk to everyone as soon as possible.

CHOOSING A LOCATION

TRAVEL IS MOST SATISFYING IF you have researched your destination thoroughly and know why you are going there. A backpack offers you unlimited freedom to participate in the activities described below. Having decided on an activity, you can research which location has the most exciting options.

Ski Touring
Some ski-touring areas are well organized, with trails, equipment rental, and guides. In other areas you may be on your own.

Canyon Hiking
Hiking in an unusual, spectacular landscape is an attractive option. Try to find people who have been to the destination you are considering, and get their opinion. Even on organized tours, guides can mistake the route or conditions, so make sure you understand what is planned. Be prepared to back out if you are not satisfied.

Exploring by River
Some countries offer excellent facilities for river exploration. Always check the boat, equipment, and life jackets thoroughly before departing.

Rock Climbing
Rock climbing with a heavy backpack is very demanding. Get plenty of practice within range of emergency facilities before you consider climbing in a foreign country.

Hiking in Mountains
Search in guidebooks for photographs of mountains that you would really like to visit. Be wary of the effects of altitude, however, and be firm about staying within your capabilities.

Mountain Biking
Publications for bikers recommend routes on which biking is welcomed, rather than prohibited by law.

Island Hopping
Visiting groups of islands by boat is easy with a backpack. Be sure you carry fresh water and a windproof garment.

Mountaineering
Some areas of the Himalayas provide good facilities for hikers and climbers, although this can also bring crowding.

Jungle Hiking
Hiking through rainforest offers incomparable sights of birds, animals, and spectacular scenery, with hidden rivers, waterfalls, and pools.

Desert Cycling
Deserts are not widely visited, so seek information about facilities and the people who live there before you go. Water availability is crucial; never take risks when cycling between waterholes.

Grassland Hiking
Grassland can be rewarding hiking territory in the spring, but heat and monsoon rains may make travel difficult or impossible later in the year.

Camel Trips
Look for unusual ways of seeing a country. Many people outside Australia would be surprised to learn that you can join camel trips in the desert.

TIMING YOUR TRIP

ALTHOUGH THE TIMES WHEN you are free to travel are likely to be determined by personal commitments, you should also be aware of changes and events taking place in the country of your destination. Research into the local climate, as well as the cultural and political situation, is amply repaid.

CLIMATIC FACTORS

Apart from details of temperature (both day and night) and rainfall during the period you are to spend in a location, in some areas you should learn when certain climatic events are expected.

The Rainy Season
Southerly winds bring high rainfall and the uniquely wet monsoon climate. The southwest monsoon blows from the Horn of Africa to India and equatorial Southeast Asia; the southeast monsoon blows northwest into Asia from the South Pacific.

The Windy Season
Typhoons and hurricanes are circular winds that rise from regions north and south of the equator. Summer typhoons occur in the Pacific and China Seas, winter hurricanes in the Caribbean Sea and the Gulf of Mexico.

Visibility
A season of very fine, clear weather often follows the monsoon. During this period, which may extend for months, photographic conditions are markedly better than at other times.

ALTITUDE

In the summer heat, the thin air at high altitude offers little protection against direct sunlight, and the air is dry, dehydrating the body. If you have a heart or respiratory problem, consider a winter visit and avoid flying directly to high-altitude places.

NATURAL ATTRACTIONS

Always visit a country when something significant, beautiful, or interesting is happening. Locals are pleased to help a traveler who has come to see the positive things their country has to offer.

Autumn Colors
Areas such as the northeastern United States are renowned for their autumn foliage. However, facilities and accommodations are likely to be busy.

Alpine Flowers
Freshly mown hay and alpine flowers smell and look better than snow, and on summertime mountain walks you can also use skiers' chairlifts.

Migrating Animals
Outstanding moments in the wildlife calendar can be a highlight of a backpacking trip. Observation of large herds is safest carried out in the vehicles of a reputable tour operator.

SOCIAL FACTORS

Always find out what is going on in a country before you book your flight. Clearly, a country at war is to be avoided, while visitors are almost always made welcome at times of celebration.

Religion
Some events, such as the Ramadan fast in Moslem countries, impose restrictions on believers that also affect travelers indirectly.

Civil War
If your destination country becomes a scene of armed warfare, do not go. The risk of being taken hostage or being caught in crossfire is too serious to ignore.

Festivals
Participating in a major festival is an exciting way to meet local people, but be prepared for higher prices than normal and scarce accommodations.

STAYING HEALTHY

KEEPING YOURSELF HEALTHY is your most important responsibility when traveling. Have full dental and medical checkups before you leave home, ensuring that your vaccinations are still effective. Take a course in first aid, and carry a first-aid kit for treating minor complaints.

BASIC FIRST-AID KIT

First aid saves lives and stabilizes a victim for the journey to proper medical care. Safety pins should be included in your kit to secure dressings and emergency bandages improvised from strips of clothing.

CREPE BANDAGE   GAUZE BANDAGE   GAUZE DRESSING

Bandages
You can use bandages to keep dressings in place, bind wounds closed, and splint broken limbs to prevent further damage.

LIMB BANDAGE   DIGIT BANDAGE

Painkillers
Save your painkillers for emergencies.

Scissors
Buy the best-quality pair that you can find.

Adhesive Bandages
Use these to prevent dirt from infecting wounds. Adhesive bandages over blisters may need tape to keep them in place.

Safety Pins
Use these for securing bandages and as temporary sutures.

Antiseptic
Use antiseptic wipes to clean wounds. Antiseptic cream promotes healing.

Triangular Bandage
A broken arm may be supported in a sling made from a large bandage.

Gauze
Gauze pads absorb blood from wounds.

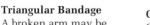

ANTISEPTIC WIPE   ANTISEPTIC CREAM

CORN PADS

Corn Pads and Felt
A corn pad or a patch of foot felt helps to prevent a small blister from becoming a major problem. Cut foot felt to fit over the sore spot. You can secure the felt in place with an

FOOT FELT

VACCINATION REQUIREMENTS

Check your vaccination record at least three months before travel. Some vaccines, such as the MMR (measles/mumps/rubella), may require a booster dose. If in any doubt, repeat the vaccination.

Zone 1: **Europe, North America, Australia, New Zealand, Japan** Tetanus only.

Zone 2: **North Africa** Typhoid, tetanus, and polio. Gamma-globulin prophylaxis is recommended against hepatitis A for visitors to the Mediterranean Coast and sea bathers.

Zone 3: **Africa** All Zone 2 vaccines, plus yellow fever and/or meningitis vaccines, and rabies vaccine for travel in rural areas.

Zone 4: **Middle East** All Zone 2 vaccines, plus rabies and meningitis for visitors to Mecca.

Zone 5: **Asia** All Zone 2 vaccines, plus rabies and Japanese B encephalitis. Meningitis vaccine for visitors to India and Nepal.

Zone 6: **Mexico, Central America, and South America** All Zone 2 vaccines, plus yellow fever for Panama and the Amazon basin. Rabies vaccine for rural areas.

Zone 7: **Caribbean and Pacific Islands** All Zone 2 vaccines. They are particularly important for Haiti and the Dominican Republic.

USEFUL TIPS

- Always carry certificates of vaccination with you, pinned securely into your passport.
- Some countries require an International Certificate of Vaccination against yellow fever, particularly if you are entering or passing through the yellow-fever zones in Africa and South America. Check the regulations of every country you intend to visit.
- To eliminate the risk of contracting HIV from a reused hypodermic needle, carry a pack of sterile needles for use in an emergency.

MALARIA

Antimalarial treatment must start up to two weeks before departure to be effective. Your destination governs which antimalarial drug you will be prescribed. Be aware that bites from *Anopheles* mosquitoes transmit the disease. Continue to take your medication for at least four weeks after leaving the zone of malaria risk.

ANOPHELES MOSQUITO

GETTING FIT

BACKPACKING TAKES STAMINA, so be sure to start training early. Stretching exercises help to develop suppleness, and aerobic exercises such as swimming improve the efficiency of your heart and lungs. Working out with weights increases the power of your legs and arms, shoulders, and back.

CHECKING YOUR FITNESS

The Step Test below determines the efficiency of your heart and lungs and will give you a good indication of your general fitness level. The step should be no more than 8 in (20 cm) high. Perform 24 step-ups per minute for three minutes, placing the entire foot flat on the step each time, with the other foot flat on the ground. Now rest for 30 seconds, then take your pulse at the wrist. Count the beats for 15 seconds, then multiply by four to get a heart rate per minute. Finally, check your heart rate against the table below.

1 Place your whole foot carefully on the step or box.

2 Keeping your knee and leg straight, thrust your body upward.

3 Maintain your balance, then step back down. Step up using the other leg.

AGE (years)	20–29	30–39	40–49	50+
RATING	BEATS PER MINUTE AFTER EXERCISE			
Men				
Excellent	under 76	under 80	under 82	under 84
Good	76–85	80–87	82–89	84–91
Average	86–101	88–103	90–105	92–107
Poor	over 101	over 103	over 105	over 107
Women				
Excellent	under 86	under 88	under 90	under 92
Good	86–93	88–95	90–97	92–99
Average	94–110	96–112	98–114	100–116
Poor	over 110	over 112	over 114	over 116

ARM AND SHOULDER STRETCH

1 Swing both arms gently backward and upward.

2 Swing your arms forward and up, touching your ears.

3 Rotate one arm forward. Repeat with the other arm.

4 Swing each arm alternately backward.

CHEST AND SHOULDER STRETCH

1 Lift your elbows up high and hold your forearms horizontally.

2 Pull your elbows back as far as possible, and then repeat.

3 On the third pull, straighten your arms out fully and horizontally from your sides.

WAIST STRETCH

1 Stand with your forearms high and elbows held up at chin level.

2 Twist your upper body from the waist to one side as far as possible, and then repeat.

3 On a third twist, throw your leading arm out straight. Repeat.

STOMACH TONER

1 Lie with your knees bent and your thumbs just touching your ears.

2 Lift your shoulder, pointing your elbow at the opposite knee.

ARM TONER

1 Lie face down, keeping body straight and palms flat on the floor.

2 Straighten your elbows and thrust upward, keeping your body in a straight line.

Continued on next page

BUILDING YOUR STAMINA

Physical fitness reduces your susceptibility to injury on the trail. Training develops your stamina, strength, and agility, while giving you an awareness of your physical limitations that prevents you from being overambitious. An effective training program must be gentle and progressive, slowly building from strength to strength.

Watch television or listen to radio to prevent boredom

Adjust saddle so that your legs are stretching without straining lower back

Vary your posture by bending or straightening arms

Swimming
Swimming develops all-round fitness, although the arms and shoulders benefit at the expense of the legs. Supported by water, the body is at little risk of strain or injury. Swimming is an aerobic exercise because the heart and lungs are able to accelerate their action sufficiently to satisfy the working muscles' increased oxygen requirements.

Exercise Cycling
An exercise bike provides a good workout for the legs, at the same time developing cardiovascular (heart-lung) efficiency. Exercise cycling is effective for warming up and stretching the legs before other activities. Continue long enough to induce a sweat, building up gradually to longer cycling sessions.

CARRYING YOUR BACKPACK

Get used to carrying your backpack on walks, building up both the distance you walk and the weight you carry. Wear boots and walk briskly. Avoid running with your pack because you could damage your knees and back. Even highly trained military personnel, who sometimes jog while carrying heavy equipment, will do so only downhill or on flat ground, and on reasonably predictable terrain.

Aim to carry the minimum, with your backpack always packed correctly

Use sternum strap to spread weight from shoulders across your chest

DEVELOPING STRENGTH

A backpack places strain on your back, shoulders, knees, and feet, affecting your balance and increasing the risk of ankle and knee injuries. Overall muscular strength minimizes weariness and protects you against injury. Start training well before your trip.

Upper Body
Weight-training exercises develop specific sets of muscles, while exercising others to a lesser extent. The bench press develops the chest, but also the upper back and arms.

Arms
Arm curls help develop arm and shoulder strength. Set up a training schedule, and perform each exercise with weights light enough to enable you to do all the set repetitions.

Chest
Exercises on multigym equipment, such as this chest movement, should first be performed with easy weights to condition muscles and ligaments. Weights that are too heavy can tear muscle away from the sternum.

Legs
Begin with legs fully bent, using a weight that you can easily move. Exercise the calves separately, using slightly heavier weights.

Extend the legs fully each time.

PRACTICE WALKS

Use practice walks to accustom yourself to the fit of your backpack, outdoor clothing, and boots. Begin by walking only a couple of miles. When walking for an afternoon comes easily, practice your navigation skills, starting in a familiar area.

TRAVELING OUT

INTERNATIONAL AIR TRAVEL CAN be tiring and stressful, and you may face an additional long journey when you reach your destination. Arrive early at the airport, bring good books to divert you, and be sure to carry adequate cash in the currency of your destination to cover expenses on arrival.

BEATING JET LAG

Crossing time zones upsets your sleeping pattern, particularly when you travel from west to east and come forward in time. Crossing the International Date Line, you gain or lose a day.

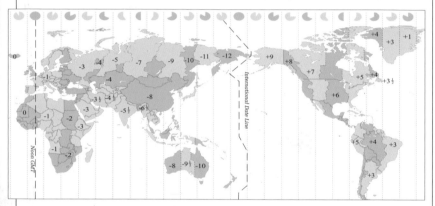

Crossing Time Zones
The map *(above)* relates local times to noon, Greenwich Mean Time (GMT) in London. The symbols *(above the map)* show how, traveling around the world from London, you cross 24 time zones, losing or gaining an hour in each zone as you travel eastward or westward toward the International Date Line. The numbers indicate how many hours must be added or subtracted in each of the time zones to reach GMT.

Use an eyeshade to block out light and help you sleep

Setting Your Watch
As soon as your aircraft takes off, the airport time *(above)* can be disregarded. What really matters is the time at your destination, so find out what it is and set your watch accordingly *(left)*.

Sleeping on Schedule
Wearing an eyeshade can help you to sleep in the aircraft during the hours that correspond to nighttime at your destination.

ORGANIZING YOUR EQUIPMENT

For air travel, one large, zipped bag is safer than baggage consisting of many loose items *(right)*. Before your trip, list your belongings, including the serial numbers of cameras and other valuables. Weigh your equipment – it may prove economical to buy a ticket with a generous baggage allowance. Label your baggage with your name, home or forwarding address, and international telephone number. Pack separately any restricted items, such as long knives, that you wish to take on board.

COMPLETING THE JOURNEY

After a smooth international flight, arrival at a far-flung airport can be disorienting, especially when you are dependent on less reliable forms of transport to continue your journey. Prearranging your transportation will save you plenty of time, effort, and anxiety.

Ships and Ferries
When boarding a craft, check whether there are reclining racks for sleeping and see how people are storing their luggage. Never lose sight of your belongings. Local journeys can be tedious, so strike up conversations with local people and carry plenty of provisions.

Railroads
Railroad journeys are often inexpensive and train travel can be very enjoyable. Steam locomotives still operate in some areas – beware of cinders getting into your eyes if you put your head out of the train window.

Buses
Developing countries have extensive networks of bus routes and many remote areas are accessible only by bus. Assure yourself that the driver is sober and competent and that your baggage is safely stowed.

Boats
Life jackets are not always available, but wear one if possible. While local boatmen are usually skilled, speak up if you think the boat is overloaded.

MEETING THE PEOPLE

MAKING CONTACT WITH PEOPLE who are very different from yourself is a great pleasure of traveling. Do not have preconceptions of how they should be, but respect them for who they are. Remember that airports and tourist resorts attract con artists, who are never representative of a country's people.

RELIGIOUS CODES

In many countries, religion plays a central role in people's personal, cultural, and political lives.

Western travelers, who are often unaccustomed to religious rituals, should be careful not to offend.

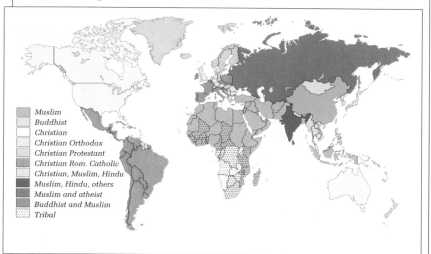

- Muslim
- Buddhist
- Christian
- Christian Orthodox
- Christian Protestant
- Christian Rom. Catholic
- Christian, Muslim, Hindu
- Muslim, Hindu, others
- Muslim and atheist
- Buddhist and Muslim
- Tribal

World Religions
The map above broadly indicates the dominant religions around the world. Although Christianity, Buddhism, Islam, and Hinduism enjoy numerical superiority in specific regions, each region is also populated by pockets of adherents to sects or alternative faiths. For the visitor, knowledge of the beliefs held by the majority of the population is vital to understanding how people live – and their attitudes.

Religion and the Traveler
In some countries, religious customs are enforced by law. Travelers are often required to conform to these laws, and can be prosecuted and punished if they do not. Western travelers, who are mostly accustomed to religious tolerance, may be shocked to experience restrictions imposed by religion at first hand. Always honor the customs of the people you meet, particularly those related to holy places and temples *(left)*.

LOCAL AUTHORITIES

Getting something you need, such as a permit, from people in authority may require persistence. Minor officials may genuinely fail to understand your problem, or say no because they are powerless and do not wish to lose face.

Police and the Military
Policemen and militia will often help a foreign traveler if they are not preoccupied with their duties, and if your manner is positive and polite.

Local Leaders
In some rural areas, you can improve your stay by paying your respects to the local chief and allaying suspicions the community may have about you.

 USEFUL TIPS

• Never criticize any aspect of a country in front of officials. Even if they agree, your outspokenness lessens their status. Cooperation requires mutual respect.
• Be patient with officials. Getting annoyed reduces your chances of making yourself understood.

INTRODUCING YOURSELF

Adopt a friendly formality when meeting people; informality can appear ignorant and rude, or as taking liberties. Work hard to evaluate the people you meet, and always show respect, particularly to elders and women.

Asking Directions
Interesting conversations usually begin with a simple exchange, such as when you ask for and are given directions.

Eating with People
People are often astoundingly generous. An invitation to share a meal is an offer of friendship.

Blending In
By adopting local attire, you disguise a potentially divisive difference between you and the people around you.

ACCLIMATIZATION

THE NATURAL RHYTHMS of the human body are disrupted by international air travel. After crossing time zones and jumping from one climate into another, your body needs time to adjust to the new conditions. Treat yourself to good food, and rest thoroughly before undertaking anything strenuous.

ADJUSTING YOUR DIET

Your body will acclimatize most rapidly if you restrict yourself to drinking clean water and eating fresh foods. Do not take risks with your diet until your digestion has adapted to the new conditions.

Choosing Drinks
Long flights are dehydrating. On arrival, drink plenty of sterilized water, or ask for bottled water, opening the bottles yourself to check that suspect local water has not been substituted. Avoid alcohol, coffee, and tea because they are diuretics and increase water loss in urine.

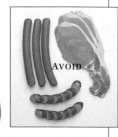

Choosing Food
A vegetarian diet reduces the risk of stomach upset, provided that the vegetables are fresh, well washed in sterile water, peeled, and boiled. Avoid salted meats until your digestion is fully readjusted to the new conditions. Fish should be bought fresh before sunrise in hot countries. Patronize clean, hygienic restaurants.

HEAT AND COLD

In hot places, always have safe drinking water with you and sip constantly. In the cold, your appetite increases, prompting you to eat more and causing you to put on an insulating layer of fat.

Hot Days
In hot countries, people are most active in the early morning and evening when it is coolest. If possible, stay out of the sun at midday and cover your head and neck with an Arabian shamaag or a wide-brimmed hat. Wear sunglasses with protective lenses.

Shamaag bunches up into a thick, insulating scarf

Shamaag extends to protect shoulders and arms from sun

Cold Nights
Whereas the body adapts to heat by stepping up sweat-gland activity, improved insulation is its only defense against cold. On cold nights, an Arabian shamaag doubles as a warm scarf to insulate the neck.

Making Shade
When crossing open deserts or exposed mountains, it may prove difficult to find natural shade. One solution is to use your lightweight emergency foil blanket as a portable source of shade. The foil reflects the sun's rays, making it relatively cool under the blanket, and the shade also rests your eyes from the glare of the sun.

ADJUSTING TO ALTITUDE

The best way to acclimatize to high altitude is to ascend gradually and lightly laden, thereby undertaking gentle exercise while slowly gaining altitude. The body compensates for the thinning air by producing extra red blood cells that increase oxygen uptake. If altitude sickness does occur, descending to a lower altitude is the natural remedy, although drugs such as diamox (acetazolamide) can be used safely to treat symptoms.

Knowing the Hazards

As a backpacker, you have plenty of opportunity to participate fully in the lifestyle of the countries you visit. However, in foreign countries you must be alert for unfamiliar hazards to your health, and take extra precautions to avoid health problems that could ruin your adventure.

Foods

Sampling exotic local foods is one of the excitements of travel. However, never buy if you see evidence of lax hygiene in a restaurant or at a food stall – your health could pay a high price.

Street Foods
Avoid wares that are exposed to flies or other sources of contamination *(left)*. Buy food that is cooked in front of you at a high temperature, perhaps deep fried in very hot oil, or cooked in water that is boiling vigorously.

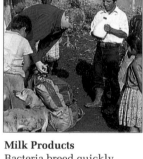

Milk Products
Bacteria breed quickly in milk and milk products. After washing your hands, boil the milk and keep it in a sterilized container.

Prepared Foods
Avoid sliced raw fruit or vegetables, both in the street *(above)* and in hotels, because they may be contaminated. It is safer to buy foods whole.

Fruit and Vegetables
Prepare and cook vegetables and fruit yourself, peeling them just before you eat them. Thin-skinned fruit and leafy vegetables should be boiled with added sterilizing powder. Eggs are safe if they are fresh and their shells are intact.

DRINKING AND BATHING

No water, not even that in high mountain streams, can be relied upon to be safe to drink without sterilization. Bathing also incurs risk because even a relatively minor contaminant upstream, such as a dead animal, could be releasing bacteria into the water.

AVOID

Beverages
Bottled or canned drinks should be consumed cold, but avoid ice – it may be frozen contaminated water.

 WARNING

Always wear some sort of protective footwear in the tropics to prevent schistosoma and other organisms from burrowing into your feet. Get into the habit of wearing sandals for showers.

Bathing
Before entering a river, check upstream for sewage outfalls or other sources of harmful microorganisms.
Try not to swallow any water. Never dive without first checking the depth and looking for underwater hazards.

OTHER HAZARDS

Travelers overseas sometimes forget that risk-taking can have more severe consequences than at home. Whether or not it accords with your nature, it is usually best to err on the side of caution.

Dentistry
Dentists in many countries may not be as skilled or well equipped as your own, and a visit should be contemplated only in the event of long-term, intolerable toothache.

Animals
Contact with both domestic and wild animals is best avoided altogether. Even pets, which may actually be unused to being handled, can inflict a deep bite that is slow to heal.

 WARNING

Travelers seeking romance should take a supply of condoms because the human immunodeficiency virus (HIV) is now widespread in many parts of the world. In some hospitals, HIV-infected hypodermics are reused for blood transfusions. It is safer to provide your own intravenous kit.

2
EQUIPMENT AND TECHNIQUES

Buying outdoor gear can be bewildering and expensive, especially if you have never camped before and are buying everything at once. Start looking early and research your needs very thoroughly. Some sales staff have little practical experience of life outdoors, so trust your instincts, talk to other backpackers, and examine the equipment for flaws before buying. Be miserly in the extreme because it is easy to be "talked up" into buying unnecessarily expensive items.

CLOTHING

THE BEST FABRICS OFFER INSULATION from the cold and allow your body to shed heat and moisture. Loose-fitting garments also help prevent overheating and excessive perspiration, and permit freedom of movement. Some fabrics offer less insulation when wet and require a separate waterproof layer.

THE LAYERING PRINCIPLE

Multiple layers of thin clothing are far more effective than a few thick layers at trapping air against your skin to be warmed by your body heat. Body temperature can be controlled by adding or removing layers, and by opening zippers and buttons to vent your garments.

The Core Layer
The core layer of clothing, which lies next to the skin, should consist of a cotton vest or a long-sleeved, thermal top. This garment should be close-fitting, but not tight or constricting. It should be made of a material that will absorb perspiration and "wick" it away from the skin (transfer it to the outside of the material). This layer must be kept as clean as possible, to prevent a build-up of dirt that may clog up its pores and prevent wicking.

The Second Layer
The second layer should be loose-fitting, but with the potential for keeping the blood vessels of the neck and wrists protected and warm. It can consist of a zipped-up top with a polo neck, or a shirt with a collar, sleeves that can be rolled up, and cuffs that can be buttoned. In hot weather, this layer may be the outside one, with perhaps just a windproof shell *(see page 34)*. A zippered polo neck can be vented in warmer weather.

The Third Layer
The third layer should be a woolen pullover or light fleecy jacket. If you are on the move, even in the Arctic, this layer is best removed to prevent you from becoming overheated. You can vent your insulated parka *(see page 35)* if you are still hot. When you stop to rest, you should replace the middle layer before you start to feel the cold. This layer can act as the outside one in mild, temperate weather, although you should keep a waterproof garment on hand.

The Outer Layer
The outer layer should be a jacket that is either wind-resistant or waterproof, or both, depending on the climate in which you are traveling. In the Arctic, a padded, windproof parka is indispensable for protection against cutting winds. You must be able to vent the jacket, however, to avoid potentially dangerous overheating and excessive perspiration. In temperate areas, rain is the main problem, although you can wear a waterproof shell over the jacket.

Underpants

In mild weather, this layer can consist of cotton shorts. Thermal underwear, especially the longjohn type with elastication at the ankle, tends to be necessary only in below-freezing temperatures, unless you anticipate long periods of inactivity. In Arctic conditions, an impermeable "groin patch" prevents windchill in that area, particularly when skiing. Wet pants take longer to dry if you are wearing long underwear underneath. Waterproof over-pants can cause discomfort by preventing the evaporation of perspiration.

Pants

Pants must allow freedom of movement and should be made of a fabric that will dry quickly if it gets wet. In very wet conditions, using a pair of braces prevents a belt from chafing the waist. Waterproof over-pants can be worn to protect your legs from driving rain *(see page 35)*, but pants made from an impermeable fabric may cause you to become overheated. In very cold conditions, quilted over-pants should be zipped over pants and boots to provide added protection, particularly when resting after a period of strenuous activity.

CHOOSING CLOTHING FABRICS

Wool is a natural fiber that has insulating properties even when it is wet, retaining warmth until virtually soaked. It smoulders, rather than burns, when exposed to flames.

Wool absorbs a lot of moisture and becomes heavy when wet. A soaked woolen garment takes time to dry. Worn next to the skin, it can make the skin itch. It can shrink when washed.

Cotton is hard-wearing and able to "breathe," absorbing moisture. It is a good choice for underwear and any other item of clothing, such as a bandanna, that is worn next to the skin.

Cotton is heavy when wet, and items can shrink if dried too fast. A wrinkled cotton garment can cause discomfort if worn against the skin. Cotton is not windproof, may tear, and burns easily.

Fleece or Pile is used for the third layer to wick moisture away from the body while keeping it warm. Fleece or pile garments are lightweight and hard-wearing and do not absorb moisture.

Fleece or Pile is not windproof, although some garments incorporate a layer of windproof polycotton at the neck and over the chest to deal with this problem. Fleece also does not compress easily.

Synthetic, Breathable Fabrics let sweat evaporate while keeping rain out. They are usually windproof, and are therefore used as the outer garments in temperate and cold conditions.

Synthetic, Breathable Fabrics can let in water at the seams in heavy weather. Dirt may clog their pores, causing condensation to form inside the garment and making it essential to vent the garment regularly.

Continued on next page ☞

KEEPING COOL

Clothing for hot weather should be lightweight and loose-fitting. The layering principle applies here, just as much as in cold weather. Light colors reflect heat and help keep you cool, although they may provide less protection against harmful ultraviolet light than darker colors. Shorts and short-sleeved shirts are pleasant to wear in cool, cloudy conditions but otherwise may expose your arms and legs to dangerous levels of ultraviolet radiation.

Hat
A wide-brimmed hat protects the head and neck from the sun.

Core Layer
A light-colored, cotton T-shirt worn under a shirt absorbs sweat away from your skin, helping you to stay cool.

Outer Layer
A lightweight, windproof jacket worn over the top will act as the final layer, protecting you from the wind and from the cold at night. Some modern lightweight fabrics have surprisingly good insulating properties.

Second Layer
A lightweight shirt acts as the main layer. Sleeves should be rolled down for extreme heat, such as that experienced in the desert.

Pants
Pants should be loose-fitting and made of a lightweight material such as cotton. Pants with many pockets are useful for carrying vital equipment such as map and compass, keeping the hands free and reducing the need for a day jacket.

Boots
Boots should be lightweight, with uppers that allow the feet to breathe and lose heat, and tough, heavy-duty soles to insulate you from hot ground (see page 37).

PROTECTING YOUR HEAD

In cold, wet, or windy conditions, wearing a hat can prevent the loss of up to half of your body heat by convection from the head. Some hats include flaps that prevent heat loss from the neck area.

Hat can extend downward to insulate back and sides of head and neck

PAKISTANI HAT   RUSSIAN HAT

KEEPING DRY

Waterproof clothing should prevent water from penetrating into your clothing, but also allow perspiration to escape.

Hood
Hoods restrict vision and hearing, and are therefore best used only in heavy rain or strong winds, or when resting.

Jacket
Keep your jacket zipped and any fasteners secured. While walking, unzip the jacket to vent your clothing.

Pockets
When it is raining, zip up the pockets to prevent them from filling with water trickling down the arms of the jacket.

Pants
Wear waterproof pants only in heavy rain because they cause perspiration. Gaiters are an excellent substitute when walking in wet grass.

Boots
Fully waterproofed boots are uncomfortable, making the feet overheat and perspire. Gaiters and hiking boots with a sewn-in tongue are a better choice.

KEEPING WARM

In extreme cold, the skin must be well covered, but remember that trapped perspiration reduces the insulating properties of your clothes.

Head Protection
A balaclava covers the head, much of the face, and the neck.

Core Layer
A thermal vest and long underwear absorb sweat.

Middle Mittens
Wool mittens between the inner gloves and outer mittens allow you to grasp objects.

Second Layer
A polo-necked shirt should overlap the balaclava at the neck.

Inner Gloves
Inner gloves prevent the skin from sticking to frozen objects.

Middle Layer
A fleece jacket should absorb perspiration yet still trap a layer of warm air against your body.

Pants
Ski pants overlap the waist while allowing venting of the upper body. They are often worn over pants.

Outer Layer
A padded, hooded parka should have overlapping front fastenings and a shell of water-resistant, breathable fabric.

Outer Mittens
Wear heavy mittens on top of at least one pair of thinner ones.

Boots
Heavy snow boots have a plastic shell and thermal liners, which act as inner boots.

FOOTWEAR

BEFORE YOUR TRIP, BREAK IN your new footwear at home to prevent blisters. If time is short, soak leather boots and wear them wet until they dry, but do not attempt this on the trail. When out walking, inspect your feet several times each day, attending to discomfort before it becomes a serious problem.

CHOOSING YOUR FOOTWEAR

In choosing footwear, consider terrain, season, and the loads you intend to carry. Heavy-duty boots are suitable for most activities. Lightweight cross trainers must not be worn when carrying weight.

Cross Trainers
Cross trainers are comfortable but they do not offer as much protection as heavy walking boots. Wearing cross trainers constantly may soften the feet and make them susceptible to injury.

Molded foam sole for support

Fabric upper dries quickly when wet

Fabric Boots
Fabric hiking boots are suitable for walking over short distances, as long as the terrain is not rough. Fabric boots offer less protection to the feet than leather boots, but they dry out quickly after a soaking. Wearing fabric boots after a walk in heavier boots gives the feet a chance to recover from strain.

CLEANING YOUR BOOTS

1 Remove laces and inner soles and wash off all mud. Peat, in particular, contains acid that spoils leather.

2 Allow the boots to dry thoroughly, keeping them away from direct heat that could crack the leather.

3 Waterproof the dry boots, rubbing in the compound with a finger. Always store your clean boots in a cool place.

Plastic Snow Boots

Snow boots are heavily insulated. Designed to hold the foot rigid while using crampons for grip on ice or snow, they can make walking feel awkward. Inside the tough plastic shells are separate thermal boots that insulate your feet against the frozen surface. You can wear these inner boots inside your tent.

Porous suede protects feet while letting them breathe

Nonslip cleats for walking in snow

Desert Boots

With tough soles and lightweight suede uppers, desert boots allow the feet to breathe while keeping hot sand out. High sides protect the ankles from thorny scrub, and give some support. The boots dry slowly if soaked.

Jungle Boots

Designed for a wet environment, jungle boots have rubber soles and quick-drying canvas uppers. Special instep vents allow water to be squirted out after wading.

Hiking Boots

These boots are a compromise between weight, durability, and protection. They have strong, cleated soles and hardwearing, water-resistant, leather uppers. The ankle has padded support.

Continued on next page ☞

WATERPROOFING PRODUCTS

Most types of footwear benefit from waterproofing treatment. Leather boots should be waterproofed gradually and repeatedly as part of the wearing-in process. Wax-based products are excellent, although silicone is more effective than wax at preventing leather from cracking in extremely cold conditions.

SILICONE-TYPE SPRAY

WAX-TYPE SPRAY

WAX

CARING FOR YOUR FEET

Your feet bear both your weight and that of your load. Therefore, you must harden your feet by wearing in your boots properly, and also pay attention to their welfare throughout the day.

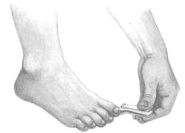

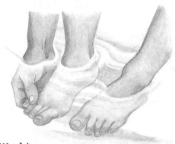

Cutting Toenails
Using a large clipper, cut your toenails short and straight across. Long toenails may tear off or cause bruising of the ends of the toes. They also increase wear on the toes of your socks.

Washing
Feet always sweat in thick socks and hiking boots, encouraging the growth of microbes. Wash your feet, preferably with soap, at least once every day, cleaning your toenails thoroughly.

Drying
Dry your feet rigorously with a rough towel or rag. After drying, expose your feet to the sun and fresh air, taking care to avoid sunburn.

Powdering
Rub an antifungal foot powder in between your toes to prevent athlete's foot. To treat athlete's foot, remove any loose skin and rub in antifungal gel.

FOOT MASSAGE

A long walk carrying weight tends to spread out your feet, straining and tiring the bones, muscles, and ligaments. You can combat this effect with massage, grasping each foot with both hands and rubbing firmly with the thumbs. Massage is also good for restoring circulation and relieving the itching that poor circulation can cause.

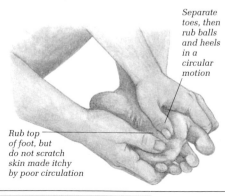

Separate toes, then rub balls and heels in a circular motion

Rub top of foot, but do not scratch skin made itchy by poor circulation

Choosing socks

Consider your expected walking conditions when choosing socks. Thick, woolen socks pad and insulate your feet against both blistering hot and frozen ground. Thin socks soak away sweat and may also be worn over thicker socks to protect them from wear.

Summer Hiking Socks
Socks for summer hiking have thick soles for insulation and padding, and thin uppers to minimize sweating. This sock type is suitable for the jungle and dries quickly after a soaking.

SUMMER SOCK

Long Socks
Knee-length woolen socks protect your legs from scratches when you are walking in shorts. Wear thin socks inside the woolen socks to soak up any sweat.

INNER SOCK

LONG SOCK

Thick sock gives additional padding and insulation

INNER SOCK

OUTER SOCK

INNER SOCK

LOOP-STITCH SOCK

OUTER SOCK

Winter Hiking Socks
Thin inner socks of breathable fabric wick moisture away from the feet. Thicker outer socks insulate the feet and pad them against your boots.

Loop-stitch Socks
Pull old socks over loop-stitch, winter-hiking socks to protect them from wear. Loop-stitch socks can be hard on the feet, so wear softer inner socks also.

Gaiters

Waterproof footwear can make the feet overheat and sweat, causing wrinkling, blisters, and fungal infections. Gaiters are preferable because they allow the feet to breathe, keep out mud and water splashes, and prevent pants from becoming soaked by wet grass. Snow gaiters stop snow from entering the tops of boots. All gaiters are easily vented.

MUD GAITERS

SNOW GAITERS

BACKPACKS AND BAGS

MOST MODERN BACKPACKS ARE FLEXIBLE in design, allowing plenty of adjustment to an individual's shape and size. Before you buy a backpack, work out how large it needs to be. You should aim to get everything you need inside the pack, without strapping anything onto the outside.

FITTING A BACKPACK

1 With a new or unfamiliar pack, weighted with a dummy load, first loosen all the straps, noting their purpose and where the tabs are located.

2 Fully extend the back adjustment system. Tightening will now be the only adjustment necessary.

3 Put on the backpack, then tighten the lower shoulder straps until the pack feels comfortable on your back and shoulders.

4 Reach behind you and locate the back adjustment. Your aim is to get the pack sitting as high as possible on your shoulders.

Tighten shoulder straps for a final adjustment

5 Tighten the waist strap. This transfers the weight from your shoulders via your pelvis to your legs.

6 Tighten the upper shoulder straps to pull the backpack into your back and raise the pack's center of gravity.

7 Tightening the shoulder straps and loosening the waist strap relieves pressure on the waist, and vice versa.

MULTIPURPOSE PACKS

With a convertible pack you can carry the weight on your back, or opt for the shoulder strap or carrying handle to blend in with other travelers. These packs also protect against pilfering and baggage-carousel damage. A stronger and cheaper alternative is to travel with your backpack stored inside a large carryall, such as a flight bag.

SHOULDER BAG

Side carrying handle

Backpack shoulder straps

Removable zipped cover

HAND LUGGAGE   UNZIPPING THE SHOULDER STRAPS   BACKPACK

DAY PACKS

A light day pack should be large enough to take all you need for a day's walk, including food, water, raingear and warm clothing, camera, maps, compass, and emergency equipment. When buying, select a strong model equipped with a frame and a padded back.

CLIMBING PACKS

Some climbing packs (no wider than the wearer's shoulders) achieve extra volume with detachable side pockets. In some designs, the pockets can be strapped together to form a day pack.

Pocket unclips and slides off for storage in camp while backpack is used for climbing

Backpack is no wider than shoulder width, allowing climber unrestricted passage through rock openings

Continued on next page ☞

LOADING YOUR BACKPACK

A loaded backpack must be well balanced, with heavy items uppermost and the weight bearing directly downward, not pulling your shoulders back or making you hunch forward. A big pack is easily filled with unnecessary equipment, so always reevaluate whether each item is essential and, ideally, has more than one use. A poncho, for example, can be used as raingear, as the roof of a temporary shelter *(see page 131)*, or as a waterproof groundsheet.

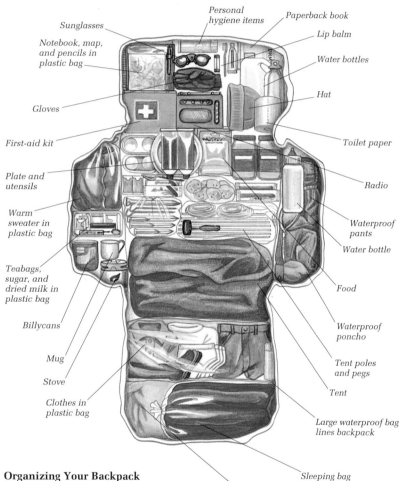

Sunglasses

Personal hygiene items

Paperback book

Lip balm

Notebook, map, and pencils in plastic bag

Water bottles

Hat

Gloves

First-aid kit

Toilet paper

Plate and utensils

Radio

Warm sweater in plastic bag

Waterproof pants

Water bottle

Teabags, sugar, and dried milk in plastic bag

Food

Billycans

Waterproof poncho

Mug

Tent poles and pegs

Stove

Tent

Clothes in plastic bag

Large waterproof bag lines backpack

Sleeping bag

Bivvy sack

Organizing Your Backpack

During the day you need access to raingear, clothing, stove, food, and water without pulling out everything else, so think through your day and pack accordingly. The contents of your backpack should be made completely waterproof to safeguard them from both wet weather and accidental immersion. A large plastic sack inside your backpack acts as an effective membrane, but your equipment should also be sorted into groups and packed in individual plastic bags.

ASSESSING YOUR LOAD

Laying out in a single place everything you want to take can help you assess whether your load is realistic. Experience will tell you how much you can carry, but aim for less than 55 lb (25 kg). When crossing rough ground, a lighter load is desirable, and 22 lb (10 kg) is a safer limit for high peaks. Make full allowance for the weight of your food and water.

BELT BAG

A belt bag keeps personal gear at hand, while bigger items are carried in a day pack. The bag cannot be worn with a backpack, however, because it prevents the use of the backpack's hip belt.

Bag Contents
What you carry will vary according to your activities. An integral water bottle is desirable in hot climates. Bear in mind that thieves can slit the fabric of belt bags, so valuables are better carried in a neck pouch in populated areas.

Water bottle in tight-fitting holder

SUNGLASSES

LIP BALM

CANDY

SKIN CARE

DOCUMENT CASE

BANDAGE

NOTEBOOK

VITAL EQUIPMENT

The safest place for vital items of equipment is hanging on strong cord around your neck, from where you can bring them into service at a moment's notice. In an accident, you may lose your backpack, bags, and clothing, but at least your neck items will be saved. Getting used to having them on your person is the best way of making sure that they are never left behind.

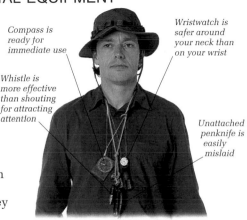

Compass is ready for immediate use

Wristwatch is safer around your neck than on your wrist

Whistle is more effective than shouting for attracting attention

Unattached penknife is easily mislaid

SLEEPING EQUIPMENT

A GOOD NIGHT'S SLEEP IS as important as hot meals. Your sleeping bag represents a haven of warmth and you should safeguard its dryness as if life depended on it – which it easily could. Keep it off bare ground, shake it hard, and turn it inside out to air whenever possible.

CHOOSING A SLEEPING BAG

Sleeping bags are manufactured for use in different conditions, so it is important that you research the average temperatures at your destination and buy a bag that is suited to the season of your trip.

Padding should be evenly distributed throughout bag

Zipper must be padded or your body will feel the cold metal

Rounded-foot Bag
The extended hood prevents heat from escaping from the head, neck, and shoulders. The zipper provides easy access to the bag, and the drawstring is tightened to keep out the cold.

Mummy Bag
With the drawstring pulled tight around the head, this style of bag minimizes heat loss. However, the lack of a zipper can make it difficult to get into and out of the bag.

SLEEPING BAG CONSTRUCTION

A down-filled sleeping bag is warm, lightweight, and compacts easily. Synthetic fillers can be slightly heavier than down, but they are often cheaper and they offer better insulation when wet.

Boxwall
The filling is distributed to minimize bunching.

Shingle
The slanted layers of fibers fill with air for insulation.

Quilt
Oval channels hold the filling, but heat escapes through stitching.

Offset Quilt
Double offset filling channels prevent heat loss through stitching.

FOOT DESIGNS

Most superior sleeping bags are constructed at the foot in ways designed to reduce heat loss and provide space for foot movement.

Box Foot
The box foot consists of two or more sections of filling that are sewn in between the upper and lower halves of the bag to eliminate heat loss at the foot. Foot movement is unrestricted.

SIDE VIEW

TOP VIEW

Fish-tail Foot
In the fish-tail foot, the upper and lower halves of the bag are sewn together vertically to allow upward foot movement. Insulation of this construction is not as effective as that of the box foot design.

SIDE VIEW

TOP VIEW

REPAIRING YOUR BAG

If your sleeping bag is torn, you should repair it immediately to prevent the damage from getting worse. A wide adhesive tape is useful for temporarily sealing a tear until you are able to sew it up properly. You can patch a tear in a bag with pieces of its stuff sack, which is often made of the same type of material.

The colors of thread can match those of your equipment

A pincushion keeps pins, safety pins, and needles in one place where you can find them

You need sharp scissors for cutting patches without spoiling or wasting the fabric

SLEEPING ACCESSORIES

Even the most expensive sleeping bag will not completely insulate body parts in contact with cold ground. Sleeping mats greatly improve insulation, as well as providing a barrier against damp.

Sleeping Mat
A mat insulates your sleeping bag from cold, wet ground. Some inflatable mats also contain plastic foam to provide support in the event of a puncture.

Liner
A cotton liner keeps a layer of air between you and your sleeping bag. It saves wear on the sleeping bag and is simpler to wash than the bag itself.

Inflatable Pillow
Not an essential item, a pillow is a useful sleeping aid during long-distance journeys in aircraft.

Space Blanket
This lightweight foil blanket is a vital sleeping aid in an emergency. The foil is windproof and conserves heat by reducing the amount of heat-carrying moisture (perspiration) that is carried away from the body. The foil also reflects away direct sunlight.

YOUR TENT

WITH MANY TYPES OF lightweight tent from which to choose, you must think carefully about how the advertised qualities of each tent are likely to meet your needs. Ideally, borrow different models from other people and try them out for the purpose you intend over several days.

FEATURES OF A TENT

The ridge tent is the best-proven tent type, with two poles, a ventilated inner tent, a built-in groundsheet, and a waterproof outer flysheet. Dome tents are also popular in the US.

Impermeable flysheet is stretched tight over poles and inner tent

Front pole is tall enough to allow comfortable exit from and entry to the tent

Rear pole is shorter than front pole so that back of tent presents small face to wind

Full-length zipper allows you to close the porch flap at night, or open it when you are cooking

Waterproofing of flysheet may get sticky when heated by sun, so allow to cool before packing

Adjustable guylines stretch and support the inner tent and poles

Thick elastic tapes keep flysheet pegged down and taut

Small porch provides a sheltered cooking area and a storage space for keeping backpacks dry

Strong, impermeable groundsheet keeps surface damp out of tent

Inner tent may not be necessary in warm regions, except in winter

Ridge Tent
A ridge tent can withstand bad weather and is easily erected in any terrain.

SELECTING YOUR TENT

Weight is very important when choosing a tent, but you must also consider strength, size, and design. In high winds, ridge tents are very stable; dome tents must be firmly pegged down.

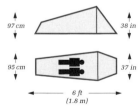

97 cm — 38 in
95 cm — 37 in
6 ft (1.8 m)

Two-man Ridge Tent
A two person, wedge-shaped ridge tent has space for cooking and storage under the flysheet.

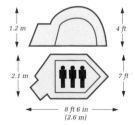

1.2 m — 4 ft
2.1 m — 7 ft
8 ft 6 in (2.6 m)

Three-man Dome Tent
Flexible poles give this dome tent more headroom than a comparable ridge tent.

TYPES OF TENT

Choose a tent that is well suited to the expected conditions. Ridge tents may be used anywhere, while a geodesic dome better withstands strong winds and heavy snow. Tents with external poles are easier to pitch in high winds than those with internal poles. In extreme weather, two-hooped tents may prove unstable.

Horizontal-ridge Tent
Similar to the wedge-shaped ridge tent, the horizontal-ridge version has a horizontal roof pole and two ends of the same height. This gives additional headroom but sacrifices the streamlining against wind afforded by the wedge shape.

Dome Tent
A dome tent necessitates firm pegging in wind, but inside it is less cramped than the interior of a ridge tent.

Single-hoop Tent
Single-hoop tents are lightweight, provide ample living space, and are easy to erect in most terrains. The tent's sloping profile deflects oncoming winds.

Tunnel Tent
Tunnel tents have a frame of up to three hoops, usually with smaller hoops at each end. Tunnel tents often have entrances at both ends.

Geodesic Dome Tent
A geodesic dome tent *(foreground)* is strong, light to carry, and easy to erect or take down. Like any domed tent, it must be strongly pegged, but the arrangement of its curved, interlocking poles makes it more stable and sturdy than a simple dome. Instead of guylines, flexible poles, crossing at intervals, serve to hold the tent fabric taut.

COOKING EQUIPMENT

 HOT MEALS AND DRINKS are vital – for morale as well as nourishment. Keep stoves and cooking utensils to the minimum, unless you are part of a group or have vehicle backup. Basic equipment includes a cooking pot with lid, wooden spoon, mug and plate, and a small stove.

STOVES AND FUELS

The main considerations when choosing a stove are weight, both of stove and fuel, and availability of fuel. Gas stoves are light and easily maintained, but do not burn as hot as pressurized models.

Mini Stove
This ultra-lightweight stove burns a butane/propane mixture that cannot be used in temperatures below freezing. It is intended only for small pots and pans.

Multifuel Stove
A very popular stove around the world, this model will cook a meal on kerosene, unleaded gasoline, or aviation fuel.

General-purpose Stove
This fast-burning stove is for all-around use, and has foldaway supports for cooking with large pans.

Foldaway support

Nonpressurized Stove
This popular stove burns methyl alcohol and has a windshield, as well as pans that pack away together. There are no mechanical parts to break down and the stove provides stable pan support.

FUELS FOR STOVES

SOLID FUEL

Your fuel bottles must be easily distinguishable from your water bottles so that there is no risk of mixing them up. They must be absolutely free from leaks, since leaking fuel could pollute food and rot clothes and equipment. Camping gas cylinders cannot be carried in aircraft, and may not be available at your destination.

KEROSENE BOTTLE   GASOLINE BOTTLE   BUTANE CYLINDER

48

LIGHTING A PRESSURE STOVE

Many types of liquid fuels are used in pressure stoves. The fuel is pressurized to make it vaporize immediately on release.

The fuel lever controls the flow of fuel from the tank to the burner

Fuel is introduced into stove via a funnel into this fuel port

Use flame-adjustment lever to clear nozzle through which fuel runs before ignition

1 After undoing the pressure-lock valve, prime the stove with at least 20 good strokes of the pressure pump. Relock the valve every time you complete a set of strokes of the pump.

Smear solid fuel all the way around the burner

2 In good conditions, the stove should light immediately. When cold, the stove will require preheating with solid fuel to enable the fuel to vaporize.

3 Light the solid fuel. Once the metal of the burner has warmed up, open the fuel control lever and the burning solid will ignite the fuel. Be patient – and ready to pump if necessary.

4 Use the flame-control lever to select either a high flame to boil water, or a low one to heat up a stew. If the flame is uncertain, pump the stove to increase the pressure.

WARNING

Pressure stoves can flare up, so never lean over one, or use one for cooking inside a tent or near an unfurled flysheet. Use unleaded, filtered fuel, stored in a container that is easily differentiated from any other you carry.

Continued on next page

UTENSILS

Your pack weight is the main consideration when selecting utensils. The bare minimum is a wooden spoon, mug, cooking pot, and maybe a bowl for hot food.

A kettle, plates, and even a skillet can be added, particularly with a group. Metal utensils can heat up and burn the hands and lips, making plastic a safer choice.

Mug
A large, tough plastic mug helps to ensure that drinks are not too hot. Avoid metal or enamel mugs, which are notorious for scalding lips.

Plate
Serving a portion of food on a plate allows you to keep the rest of your meal warm in the pot.

Bowl
Food stays hot longer in a deep bowl than in a shallow one, and spillage is minimized.

KNIFE   FORK   SPOON   HOLDER

Utensils
Choose lightweight and well-made eating implements. It is unwise to share your eating implements with others because there is a risk of bacterial contamination.

Aluminum Pot
Food heats up quickly in an aluminum pan, but you must watch it carefully because it can burn easily.

Kettle
Boiling water in a kettle frees your other pans for cooking and soaking. When you have a fire, use the kettle to warm water ready for cooking.

Skillet
A lightweight aluminum skillet is probably an unnecessary item for a single walker, but carrying one is worthwhile if you are traveling in a group, or if you have the luxury of a vehicle.

COOKING POT   LID

Trusty Utensils
You can pare down your cooking equipment to just a few reliable items. The deep aluminum cooking pot, for example, with its handle taped for insulation, is ideal for cooking in extreme conditions, and the fitted lid doubles as a bowl and a reserve cooking pan.

Billycan Set
An aluminum billycan set can save valuable pack space, but be wary of taking more pans than you really need.

FOOD STORAGE

Food containers should be light and strong, preferably transparent, with wide necks and watertight lids. First calculate the quantities of the foods you intend to carry, then buy the containers you need.

Reducing the Weight
Transferring foods from heavy glass jars and bottles to virtually weightless plastic containers not only reduces your load but also safeguards your precious stores against breakage and loss. Jars with screw-on tops are best for powdered foods such as instant coffee and hot chocolate – the press-on, pull-off type of lid can easily lead to a mess when you are tired.

POWDERED MILK   HOT CHOCOLATE   INSTANT COFFEE   SUGAR

Seasonings
Small quantities of salt, pepper, herbs, and spices can be carried in 35-mm film containers, which have airtight lids. Label each one before you travel for easy identification when you start cooking.

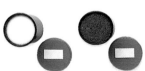

CHILI POWDER   GROUND PEPPER   MIXED HERBS

SALT

Stacking Your Foods
You can prevent losses of bulky foods that would otherwise spill or crumble in your pack by carrying them in stacked plastic tubs with firm, airtight lids.

Cut out cooking instructions from packaging and include in container

All-in-one Storage
Collect small objects, such as your packages of seasonings, together in a single container for easy accessibility. Pad out any remaining space with useful items, such as teabags.

TRAIL MIX   COOKIES

OATMEAL   RICE   HARD CANDY

PORTABLE FOODS

Dried foods enable you to carry sustenance into the wilderness without overloading your pack. Remember that they need time and plenty of water to rehydrate – never eat them dry. Canned foods add variety to your meals, but are heavy. Fresh items such as garlic are always appreciated.

DRIED FOODS

High-calorie Foods
Sweet foods are vital to maintain blood sugar levels, providing energy and keeping you warm. Suck hard candy for the extra calories they yield.

DEHYDRATED ICE CREAM

CHOCOLATE PUDDING POWDER

FRUIT-FLAVORED HARD CANDY

Breakfast Foods
Oats, muesli, and dried fruit are vital sources of energy and vitamins early in the day. Also, the fiber they contain helps speed food through the digestive tract.

DRIED FRUITS

OATS

TRAIL MIX

Beans and Pulses
Pulses and beans provide protein and fiber, and require thorough soaking before cooking. Rice contains energy-giving carbohydrate but cooks slowly.

LENTILS

KIDNEY BEANS

RICE

Trail Snacks
It is best to nibble constantly during the day to maintain energy and allay hunger, and to have a big meal at night that you can digest thoroughly while you sleep.

GRANOLA BAR

CUSTARD COOKIE

DIGESTIVE BISCUITS

CHOCOLATE BAR

CHOCOLATE COOKIE

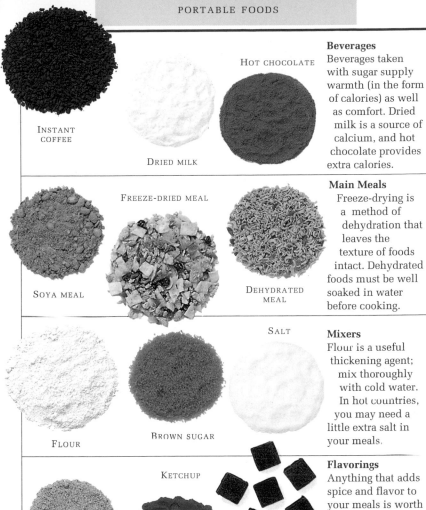

Beverages
Beverages taken with sugar supply warmth (in the form of calories) as well as comfort. Dried milk is a source of calcium, and hot chocolate provides extra calories.

HOT CHOCOLATE

INSTANT COFFEE

DRIED MILK

Main Meals
Freeze-drying is a method of dehydration that leaves the texture of foods intact. Dehydrated foods must be well soaked in water before cooking.

FREEZE-DRIED MEAL

SOYA MEAL

DEHYDRATED MEAL

Mixers
Flour is a useful thickening agent; mix thoroughly with cold water. In hot countries, you may need a little extra salt in your meals.

SALT

FLOUR

BROWN SUGAR

Flavorings
Anything that adds spice and flavor to your meals is worth carrying, especially if you plan to rely on dehydrated food. Take ingredients that will enliven and enrich your improvised sauces.

KETCHUP

GRAVY CUBES

SOUP

MEAT AND FISH

SARDINES

Although red meat and fish provide protein, all kinds of meat are difficult to keep fresh. Canned products must be consumed immediately after opening. More lightweight options are preserved meats, precooked meals, dried fish, and dried meats, such as jerky.

SALAMI

PASTA MEAL

FRANKFURTERS AND BEANS

WATER EQUIPMENT

PURE WATER IS VITAL TO HEALTH. Most water can be made fit to drink by careful filtering to remove silt and other particles, followed by chemical purification to destroy harmful organisms. If you doubt the quality of a water source, double the dose of your chemical purifier to make sure.

WATER CONTAINERS

Keep your water containers scrupulously clean to prevent recontamination of your purified water. In cold conditions, a vacuum flask is invaluable for keeping water warm overnight.

Snap-on cup

Screw-on cap

Bottle with Cup
This bottle has an integral plastic cup.

Steel Bottle
Although it is strong, a filled steel bottle can be very heavy.

Plastic Bottle
A tough, plastic bottle is ideal, but keep it away from fire.

Flask
Liquids may be kept either hot or cold in a vacuum flask.

Collapsible Canteen
Take care you do not break the tab linking the cap to the bottle, to keep from losing the cap.

Small Water Bag
Avoid laying this folding bag on the ground, where it can be easily damaged.

Belt Pouch
A belt-pouch container keeps water within easy reach, leaving your hands free.

Nozzle may be twisted open or closed

Large Water Bag
This water bag can be hung from a tree in a breeze, keeping the contents cool.

WATER PURIFIERS

Some water may be purified by boiling (for at least five minutes), but chemical sterilizers are safer and more effective. You can boil water before adding chemicals.

Iodine
Iodine can be messy to use, turns water pink, and has a distinct taste.

Tablets
Use one tablet for every 1 pint (half-liter) of water, more if the water is cold.

Pump handle

Water is pumped from container into collecting bottle

Filter lid doubles as cup

End of hose goes into impure water

Filter fits on top of canteen for filtering small amounts of water

Canteen

Filter parts fit together on water bottle

Built-in filter net with chemicals

Mini Portable Filter
When you pump the purifier's handle, impure water is sucked through chemicals in the purifier. Pure water passes out of the spout.

Cup Purifier
Impure water drips slowly through the sterilizing chemicals. Pure water collects in the canteen.

THE RISK OF DEHYDRATION

Our bodies cannot store water, so we must drink constantly. Need for water is driven by temperature, metabolism, and work. We sweat to reduce our temperature, and use water to break down food. To reduce water intake, stop eating and do little, keeping as cool as possible. Always drink enough water to ensure that urine remains clear. Cloudy or colored urine indicates the need to drink more.

THE EFFECTS OF WATER LOSS		
1–5% Lost	**6–10% Lost**	**11–12% Lost**
Thirst	Headache	Delirium
Discomfort	Dizziness	Swollen tongue
Lethargy	Dry mouth	Twitching
Impatience	Tingling in limbs	Deafness
Lack of appetite	Blue shade to skin	Darkening vision
Flushed skin	Slurred speech	Lack of feeling in skin
Increased pulse	Difficulty In breathing	Skin starts to shrivel
Nausea	Inability to walk	Inability to swallow
Weakness	Blurred vision	Death

Water Needs
Even while resting, we can lose 2 pints (more than 1 liter) of water per day in sweat, urination, and breathing. Water comprises 75 percent of our body mass, and very small losses are sufficient to affect health adversely.

CAMP NECESSITIES

IT TAKES EXPERIENCE to learn which items are essential on a journey and which are best left behind. After each trip, discard anything you did not use, and add only items you really wished you had brought. Multiuse items are particularly worthwhile choices.

USEFUL EQUIPMENT

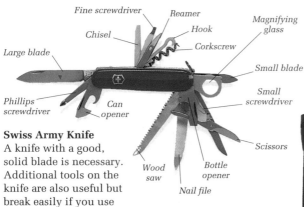

Fine screwdriver
Reamer
Chisel
Hook
Magnifying glass
Large blade
Corkscrew
Small blade
Small screwdriver
Phillips screwdriver
Can opener
Scissors
Wood saw
Bottle opener
Nail file

Swiss Army Knife
A knife with a good, solid blade is necessary. Additional tools on the knife are also useful but break easily if you use them carelessly.

Waterproof Matches
These have waxed heads to keep them dry.

Flashlight
A flashlight should be small and have a strong beam. Store it inside a plastic bag to keep out water.

Can Opener
Use a can opener to release the juices in cans before you are ready to eat the solid contents. Canned fruit juices make a pleasant appetizer.

Compass
A good compass is indispensable for any trip in wild country.

Map is folded open to show area of use

Binoculars
These should be small and robust. Keep your binoculars dry inside a plastic bag, even if the specification states that they are waterproof.

Map
A map is best kept dry in a waterproof case, folded neatly to show your present location.

WASH KIT

Good personal hygiene is doubly important in the wild. Thorough washing helps prevent minor cuts from becoming infected, and medicated shampoo prevents infestation of your hair and scalp.

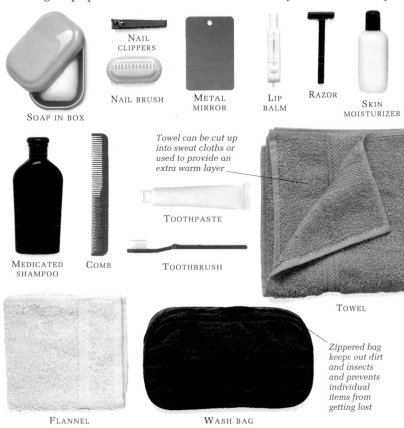

SOAP IN BOX

NAIL CLIPPERS

NAIL BRUSH

METAL MIRROR

LIP BALM

RAZOR

SKIN MOISTURIZER

MEDICATED SHAMPOO

COMB

Towel can be cut up into sweat cloths or used to provide an extra warm layer

TOOTHPASTE

TOOTHBRUSH

TOWEL

FLANNEL

WASH BAG

Zippered bag keeps out dirt and insects and prevents individual items from getting lost

SPECIAL MEDICATIONS

Whatever your destination, be prepared for the specific medical hazards there. In the jungle, for example, sharp undergrowth can inflict nasty cuts, and some jungle medical kits include antibiotic powder to treat these cuts.

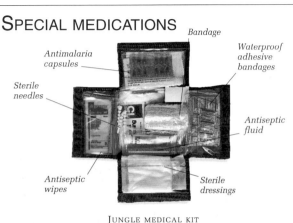

Antimalaria capsules

Sterile needles

Bandage

Waterproof adhesive bandages

Antiseptic fluid

Antiseptic wipes

Sterile dressings

JUNGLE MEDICAL KIT

YOUR SURVIVAL KIT

A BACKPACKER'S SURVIVAL KIT CONTAINS basic but vital tools designed for emergency use only. Like the first-aid kit that you should also carry, everything should fit into a single container. Remember also that, in today's world, a credit card can be the most compact and useful survival aid of all.

Fishing Hooks and Sinkers
Pack plenty of small fishing hooks, floats, and split-shot weights. Small hooks are effective for catching both large and small fish.

Fishing Line
Choose a strong line for catching fish and lashing tools.

Scalpel
This can be used for different purposes. Keep the blades in their original oiled package.

Keep saw, covered with a film of grease, inside a plastic bag

Wire Saw
A wire saw can cut most materials.

Pencil
Use this for your journal or sketch maps, or to keep notes on safe wild food in an emergency.

Thin Wire
The wire should bend easily, but not so easily that it breaks.

Safety Pins
Use these for securing your clothing, sleeping bag, or tent.

Potassium Permanganate
These crystals sterilize water and treat fungal infections.

Mirror
Looking through the hole, you can direct sunlight onto an airplane and thereby attract attention.

Sewing Items
Buy large-eyed needles and waterproof thread, and store them in a plastic bag. Large buttons are useful for securing tent flaps as well as replacing losses.

Salt
Heavy sweating plus urination can severely deplete your salt reserves, causing muscle cramps. Adding a pinch of salt to your meals should prevent cramps.

Plastic Bag
This can be used to carry water from a stream or as a head covering.

Antibiotic Tablets
These should be used only in an emergency.

Bandages
Use these to prevent abrasions from becoming infected, or to pad blisters on the feet until they can heal.

Button Compass
Luminous markings are preferable.

Water Sterilizers
Keep these as an emergency reserve supply.

Magnifying Glass
You can use a magnifying glass to start a fire. Focus sunlight onto some dry tinder; when it begins to smolder and catch fire, gradually add larger, dry materials until they ignite.

Candle
Use this for firelighting rather than as a lamp.

Matches
Matches can be waterproofed with candle wax. Scrape off the wax before striking.

Storage Tin
A small tobacco tin with a tight-fitting lid is ideal for the storage of your life-saving equipment. Seal the closed tin with tape to keep the contents dry. Always keep the tin in the same place, so that checking that you have the tin with you can become instinctive. Clearly mark the tin as your survival kit.

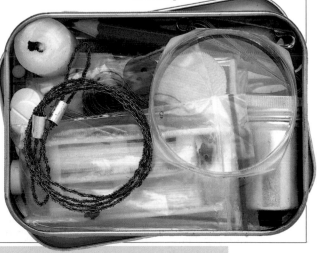

MAKING REPAIRS

REPAIR DAMAGED EQUIPMENT IMMEDIATELY – a stitch in time always saves at least nine. Before your trip, check all your equipment, even new items, for faults such as frays or loose stitching that could be finished and strengthened. Sharpen your cutting tools, because blunt blades are dangerous.

SEWING EQUIPMENT

A sewing kit is important for any medium- or long-term trip. On a short trip, most problems can be solved with either string or a roll of strong insulating tape. Keep needles dry because they can rust.

BUTTONS

CANDLE

SAFETY PINS

FABRIC PATCHES

THIMBLE   THREAD   NEEDLES

SCISSORS   WOOL

Patches used for temporary repairs to items made of fabric

TOBACCO TIN

Tin with tight-fitting lid keeps sewing items together

Assembling Your Sewing Kit
Include a thimble for pushing needles through tough material. One large darning needle is useful for repairing socks, and other needles should have wide eyes. Take thick, black or white thread, which shows up easily. To waterproof and strengthen thread, wax it by rubbing it on a candle.

MENDING A SLEEPING MAT

An inflatable sleeping mat is more compact than a foam mat, but it can be made completely useless by a puncture. It is wise to take a puncture-repair kit with you for making immediate repairs.

1 Spread rubber solution around each hole, covering an area slightly larger than the patch you intend to use. Allow the glue to dry.

2 Firmly press the patches onto the dried glue. If they do not stick instantly, try again, giving the glue more time to dry.

3 Cut large adhesive patches of tough material to provide overall protection for the individual repairs. Press down the patches firmly.

CUTTING TOOLS

A penknife is a vital item, as is a larger blade to fulfill the functions of an ax, a machete, and even a hammer. Be aware that special laws apply to the carrying of large knives when using transportation.

Kukri

Variants of the kukri knife that originated with the Gurkha infantrymen of Nepal can be bought worldwide. The kukri serves as a heavy-duty cutting tool, tackling with ease tasks such as wood chopping that are beyond most camping knives. Keep it safely in its leather sheath to avoid injury.

Back of blade is blunt, and can be used for hammering

Be sure to repair promptly any damage to wooden handle

Tip of blade is kept sharp, and is used for general cutting

Middle section of blade is not as sharp as tip, and is used for chopping

Inner curve of blade is very sharp, and is used for delicate carving and whittling

Penknife

A strong penknife is indispensable for countless small cutting tasks. Keep it secured to your body with strong cord at all times, either around your neck or waist. Always keep it sharp.

Rust will weaken serrated blade, so clean saw after cutting living wood

Wire Saw

An important item in your survival kit *(see page 58)*, a wire saw consists of twisted strands of wire, with loops for handles. It is delicate and must be used with care.

SHARPENING A KNIFE

1 Lubricate a sharpening stone with water. Stroke the knife on the stone, pushing away from you so that the blade's edge rubs against the stone.

2 After sharpening the knife on one side, feel the other side for the burr of metal turned up by the abrasion. Take care not to press too hard on the edge and cut yourself.

3 Smooth the other side of the blade, visualizing the curved burr as you sharpen and realign it to the center of the blade. The stone may need further lubrication.

4 Strop the knife (sweep it up and down) on a leather belt. This will smooth off any loose fragments of metal and help to strengthen the edge.

FINAL ADJUSTMENTS

COMFORT IN THE WILD RESULTS more from self-sufficiency and good organization than from owning top-quality equipment. Every item of equipment should be readily at hand, and you should be able to make any necessary repairs yourself, so you must carry a range of mending materials.

PREPARING YOUR EQUIPMENT

Any small adjustments you make to your equipment at home could make life easier when on the trail.

Talk to other backpackers about how they organize themselves and streamline their daily routines.

Gloves
Joining your gloves with a cord prevents a potentially disastrous loss of a glove in freezing conditions.

Zipper
Zippers can be difficult to grip. A length of cord, knotted at the end and attached to a zipper, can make the zipper easier to pull.

Elastic Bands
Looped onto your hip belt, elastic bands have many uses on the trail.

Tape
Strips of adhesive tape, stuck inside your pack, are useful for repairs.

Safety pins
Keep safety pins of several sizes inside your jacket, where they are protected from rusting.

LACING BOOTS

Boots laced with only one free lace-end are quick to tie and remove, and the end tucks away easily and safely. Also, if your boots rub, you can omit the hook or eyelet next to the sore area.

1 Tie a knot in one end. Lace with the knot on the outside of the bottom hole.

2 Lace to the top, then loop the lace around the ankle. If your boots have eyes, leave one free.

3 Feed the lace up behind the loop. With eyes, run the loop into the free eye first.

TRANSPORTING YOUR BACKPACK

The straps, catches, and buckles of a backpack are easily damaged in the course of air travel. Fitting the backpack into a tough, lightweight bag protects it from automatic carousels and indifferent handlers.

1 Insert the backpack into your tough, lightweight bag, with the straps lying uppermost for easy removal of the pack.

2 Close the bag and strap it up tightly to make it easy for baggage handlers to grip it correctly. When the bag is held from above by its handles, the backpack inside should lie flat.

USING BOOT BANDS

Wet pant-ends soak your calves, feet, and socks, causing discomfort as you walk. Having the ends tucked into your boots is not comfortable, so use boot bands to prevent them from slipping down.

1 Find two rubber bands that fit comfortably around your ankles without constricting the blood flow. If you cannot find suitable rubber bands, cut two lengths of wide elastic and stitch them into loops.

2 Put on your hiking socks (see page 39) and then fit the rubber bands (or elastic loops) over them.

3 Pull your pant-ends over the bands, then tuck all the excess fabric back under them. This creates a pair of temporary, elasticized hems.

4 Adjust the length until the pant-ends ride near the tops of your boots. The ends must not feel too tight.

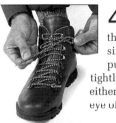

4 Tuck the end of the lace through to form a simple knot, then pull the lace tightly back against either the hook or the eye of your boot.

5 One simple knot is quite sufficient, but if you want to be certain that the boot is securely laced, make another knot and tighten the lace again.

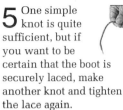

6 Tuck the excess lace back around the ankle loop, using the minimum number of turns necessary to take up the lace.

7 The loops of lace will help to support your ankle, but make sure that they are not constricting your circulation.

3
MOVING
ON THE TRAIL

B<small>Y DEFINITION, BACKPACKING IS ALL</small> about being on the trail, leading a nomadic, simple existence far from the pressures of urban life. The trail can be a well-marked path or nothing more than a compass bearing over unpredictable, even dangerous, terrain. You may prefer walking in a group, or traveling solo with only the sights and sounds of nature for company. Whatever your choice, the journey is likely to be a memorable, challenging, and exhilarating experience in its own right.

ENJOYING THE WILD

A BACKPACKING TRIP IN THE WILDERNESS offers a complete escape from the pressures of life in the industrialized world. You enter a different time zone, one that is governed by the rising and setting of the sun. So get up at dawn to start each day at one with nature, then let the day unfold.

KEEPING A JOURNAL

Recalling thoughts is every bit as important as taking photographs. Writing a journal, you engage your mind while new experiences are challenging your preconceptions. The journal builds into a lasting chronicle of how your experiences shaped your way of thinking.

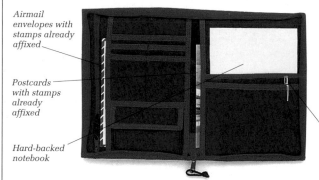

Airmail envelopes with stamps already affixed

Postcards with stamps already affixed

Hard-backed notebook

Writing Case
A writing case organizes into one place all the materials you need for your journal and for sending mail.

Pencil (with medium-soft lead) is more reliable than ball-point pen in heat or at high altitude

STAR GAZING

Free from the tyranny of electric lighting, like the ancients, you will be fascinated by the stars. Visibility is best on moonless nights, with no nearby street or house lights – and no atmospheric pollution. Using a star guide, work out in advance which stars you wish to see, because it takes about half an hour to establish good night vision and you will lose it temporarily if you need to refer to your guide with a flashlight. If you must refer to the guide while in the dark, use a dim, red-filtered flashlight and keep one eye closed – doing this speeds up the reestablishment of night vision.

OBSERVING WILDLIFE

The best time to observe wildlife is around dawn, as the birds and animals awake. Move slowly and quietly, then settle somewhere downwind of where the wildlife will appear and wait patiently.

Water Sources
Water attracts animals from great distances, particularly in late afternoon. Different species mix together, affording excellent opportunities for observation and photographs. Stay well clear of approach routes, and keep alert for signs of dangerous predators.

Nests and Breeding Sites
Do not touch animal habitats. Birds or animals may abandon their young, and larger species may attack you.

Signs of Habitation
Look for indications that animals have passed by, such as this tree damage caused by browsing elephants.

ANIMAL TRACKS

Unlike observation, which can inhibit animal behavior, tracking can teach you much about what animals actually do. Looking at the mud around waterholes is a good way to start your tracking.

Hippopotamus
A hippopotamus leaves close, parallel tracks that are deeply impressed.

Bear
A bear's tracks give a fascinating insight into its size and gait.

Jaguar
Jaguars have large feet, heavily padded for fast and silent movement.

Deer
Look for droppings that will help you identify the animal species.

Raccoon
Raccoons are mostly tree-dwellers and tracks on the ground are rare.

Hare
Hares use their hind legs for propulsion and leave distinctive tracks.

SETTING OUT

AFTER YOUR CAREFUL PREPARATIONS, do not make the mistake of pushing yourself too hard on the first day and undoing all your good work. Make the first day an easy one – start as late as you like, eat a large breakfast, and stop walking while there is still plenty of daylight for choosing your first campsite.

WALKING TECHNIQUES

Just as boots require careful "walking in" if you are to avoid discomfort and injury, walking with a backpack takes practice. A strong walking stick gives useful support on difficult terrain.

Walking Uphill
Lean forward and take short steps, placing your feet flat on the ground before pushing upward. Avoid walking on your toes.

Walking Downhill
Take short steps and move steadily, leaning backward to take the strain off your knees. Using your stick also relieves your knees.

Steep Slopes
If a slope is very steep or has a soft surface, climb it with your feet placed sideways, using your stick downhill of you as an extra support.

REST STOPS

Ten minutes after starting out, stop walking to adjust equipment and check your direction. After that, stop every 50 minutes for about 10 minutes, starting the clock as the last person sits down. In cold weather, put on warm clothing and a hat to prevent heat loss. Using your pack as a backrest, relax, have a snack, and look around.

WALKING IN A GROUP

On the trail, a group requires a leader and second-in-command. Whatever happens, the group must stick together. With a large group, the leader may wish to appoint a lead scout to go ahead and identify the best route. The second-in-command, who should be a strong walker, brings up the rear and ensures that slower walkers are not left behind.

Second-in-command, counting heads, may ask leader to slow down for stragglers

Leader supervises main party, going ahead to decide which route to take if necessary

Lead scout moves ahead, trying out different routes until the best one is found

MAKING A WALKING STICK

A strong walking stick can help you make light of the longest walk. You can prop it under your backpack during short, standing rests, steady a camera with it, or use it to beat off an attacking dog.

1 Choose and neatly cut down a strong, straight sapling with a firm fork about 4 ft (1.2 m) above where you make the cut.

2 To give your walking stick a comfortable handle, cut above the fork, selecting the thicker branch and cutting some 8 in (20 cm) above the top of the main stem. Cut off the thinner branch of the fork.

Shape surface of stick to get a smooth finish

3 A live sapling is likely to produce sap, particularly if you cut it in spring. The stick will dry out quickly if you strip off all the bark. Drying is more gradual if you leave the bark in place.

4 Smooth off the stick, particularly around the handle, to prevent any damage to your hands. Cut the bottom end off square. Most people like a stick that extends to just above waist height, but you may prefer to walk with a longer stick.

FACING DIFFICULTIES

BACKPACKING IS AS MUCH ABOUT overcoming environmental problems, such as hostile weather and treacherous terrain, as it is about enjoying nature. Being free from civilization gives you an opportunity to solve problems on your own – and enjoy the real satisfactions that true independence can bring.

COLD WINDS

Cold winds can rapidly lower local temperatures and bring sudden rain. Strong winds make movement physically strenuous and penetrate clothing, removing both heat and moisture.

Combating Cold

Always wear a hat to prevent rapid heat loss from the head and neck. When resting in a cold wind, immediately put on warm, windproof clothing: never wait until you feel cold. Sit on your backpack to prevent heat loss into the ground and hunch yourself up, hands in pockets, to conserve all your body heat.

Pull hood up over your hat and zip it up tight to conserve heat.

Sit out of wind, or with your back to it, hunched forward

Use pockets to keep hands warm, making sure that rain cannot trickle in

Backpack insulates you from ground

The Windchill Factor

Movement of cold air greatly increases its cooling effect *(see table, below)*. This phenomenon is called the "windchill factor." If you are wet, the risk of chill increases because the evaporation of moisture from your clothing is fueled by your body heat.

THE COOLING EFFECT OF WIND

SPEED	TEMPERATURE (°F)									
Calm	20	10	0	-10	-20	-25	-30	-35	-40	-45
	EQUIVALENT CHILL TEMPERATURE (°F)									
5 mph	16	6	-5	-15	-26	-31	-36	-42	-47	-52
10 mph	3	-9	-22	-34	-46	-52	-58	-64	-71	-77
15 mph	-5	-18	-31	-45	-58	-65	-72	-78	-85	-92
20 mph	-10	-24	-39	-53	-67	-74	-81	-88	-95	-103
25 mph	-15	-29	-44	-59	-74	-81	-88	-96	-103	-110
30 mph	-18	-33	-49	-64	-79	-86	-93	-101	-109	-116
35 mph	-20	-35	-52	-67	-82	-89	-97	-105	-113	-120
40 mph	-21	-37	-53	-69	-84	-92	-100	-107	-115	-123

☐ *Conditions very unpleasant; thermal outer clothing necessary*   ☐ *Skin begins to freeze if exposed to open air for a prolonged period*   ☐ *Outdoor travel is dangerous; skin can freeze in one minute*   ☐ *Exposed skin is likely to freeze in less than 30 seconds*

DIFFICULT TERRAIN

Although you should try to avoid dangerous terrain, often there is no alternative route. Movement is slowed considerably, but safety must be your main priority. Use the proper techniques, take your time, and never attempt awkward terrain without good cause.

Boulder Fields
One slip in a boulder run while carrying a heavy pack can break a leg. If you cannot make a detour, move slowly, testing each foothold.

Scree Slopes
Climb sideways on scree, using a stick or ski pole for support. Descending can be exhilarating; take hopping strides, taking care not to fall.

WATERLOGGED GROUND

Bogs and marshes can occur anywhere, even on slopes and hilltops. Always give them a wide berth when they are marked on a map. In moorland, keep a sharp lookout for sudden patches of bog.

Crossing a Bog
Make each step carefully, looking for patches of firm tussock grass. Watch where the people in front of you tread, and learn from their mistakes. Use a stick to test the ground ahead, and be prepared to run or skip lightly across dubious patches.

1 If you sink into a bog, pulling out a foot will cause you to sink deeper. Try to work out the best way to spread your weight evenly before you move.

2 Lay your backpack down on the firmest ground available. Lie back, and pull out your legs one at a time, letting the backpack support you.

3 If you can bring the backpack around to the front, you may be able to lie forward onto it and "swim" out. If not, remain still and await help.

USING ROPES

IN THE WILD, YOU NEVER KNOW when you might need to use a rope. A thick, rough, natural-fiber rope, at least 1¼ in (3 cm) in diameter, provides grip for hand-over-hand climbing, while knotting provides thinner rope with grip. Test any knots with your full weight before depending on them.

CHOOSING ROPES

Both hawser-laid and kernmantle rope can be used by backpackers. Ropes made from natural fibers resist heat better than synthetic ropes, but they can rot. Check a rope for faults before you buy it.

Three separate branches of fiber strands are twisted together

Thin, nylon filaments are twisted into small, hawser-laid cords

Hawser-laid Rope
Hawser-laid rope is strong and consists of three strands of fiber twisted together. Sisal, coconut husk, hemp, or nylon may be used.

Kernmantle Rope
Kernmantle rope has a core of thin, hawser-laid cords braided together (the kern), covered by a sheath (the mantle).

JOINING ROPES

When you need to join ropes to get a required length, the knot must be reliable and secure. Slippage can be fatal, so leave long ends. Tying a knot in the loose ends makes them even less likely to slip.

1 To tie a grapevine knot, first wrap the end of one rope around the end of the other.

2 Wrap the first end around for a second time, then poke the end back through the two complete loops that you have formed.

3 Tighten the knot. The end protruding from the knot should be at least 4 in (10 cm) long. Now repeat Steps 1 and 2 with the other end, but forming the loops in the opposite direction.

4 Pulling the two ropes brings the knots together. If the knot is tied correctly, both short ends emerge from the back of the knot.

COILING A ROPE

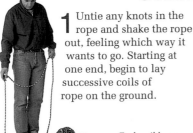

1 Untie any knots in the rope and shake the rope out, feeling which way it wants to go. Starting at one end, begin to lay successive coils of rope on the ground.

Each coil has a diameter of about 20 in (50 cm)

2 Continue to lay coils neatly and the same size, so that each coil lies slightly inside the previous one. Use your foot to hold the coils. If the surface is dirty, form the coil in your hand.

3 To secure the coil in your hand, turn back the end of the inner coil to form a loop 12–14 in (30–35 cm) long.

4 Holding the main coil in your hand, wind the end of the outer coil around it, going over the loop you made in Step 3 but leaving the loop's end free.

5 Finish winding the rope around after about 4 in (10 cm) of close lashing, leaving 1 in (3 cm) of loop protruding from the coiled lashing.

6 Pass the end of the rope through the loop. Pull the rope-end as firmly as possible to get it tight. The lashing serves as a "carrying handle" for the coil.

7 Pull the end of the rope that forms the loop. This will pull the loop under the lashing and secure it.

REPAIRING A SYNTHETIC ROPE-END

1 First, the frayed rope fibers must be melted together. Allow them to burn until they are all subsumed into the melted part. (To repair a natural-fiber rope-end, in contrast, the loose fibers must be lashed with thin cord.)

2 Having blown out the flame, wet your fingers and quickly press the hot blob into a cylindrical shape of the same diameter as the rope. If your fingers are not wet, the melted plastic may stick to your fingers and burn.

Continued on next page

TYING A BOWLINE KNOT

A bowline is used to form the loop of a lifeline because it will not slip or work itself loose. The way to tie a bowline can be remembered using the analogy of a rabbit, a hole, and a tree *(see below)*. For extra safety, a simple knot can be tied in the trailing end.

1 Make an overhand loop and bring the end up through it. (The end – the "rabbit" – comes up through the loop – the "hole.")

2 Take the end around the main rope, then back through the loop ("the rabbit comes out of the hole, goes around the tree, and then back down the hole again").

Pull both ends to tighten knot

3 Pull the end and the main rope to tighten the knot. The bowline is a useful knot, although many climbers prefer the figure-eight knot *(see below)* for lifelines.

TYING A FIGURE-EIGHT KNOT

The figure-eight (which you can tie with the rope doubled for extra strength) will not slip or work loose, yet is easy to untie. Use it to form loops, into which you can clip carabiners and other items.

1 Begin this knot by forming a small underhand loop about 2 ft (60 cm) from the end of the rope.

2 Take the loose end over the top of the rope and the loop, then up through the loop, forming a figure-eight.

3 Pull both ends to tighten the knot. This stage of the knot can be left in the end of your rope, ready for whenever a loop needs to be formed.

4 To form the loop, put the loose end of the rope around whatever you are securing it to, then firmly push it back into the figure-eight knot.

5 Bring the loose end of the rope around the outside of the figure-eight and back up through the first loop. This completes the knot shape and it is now ready for tightening.

6 Pull tight on the finished loop and the long end of the rope. This knot is very reliable and is often used in climbing. It will not work loose, yet may easily be undone.

ROPING UP

Roping up ensures that a climber who falls can always be rescued. In the top position, you must be secure against being pulled down should your partner fall – two victims cannot help each other.

Always have three points of contact with the rock

1 Carry the rope coiled over your shoulder, looking upward for a good belay (fixing point).

2 At the belay, tie the trailing end of the rope around your waist with a figure-eight knot. Leave several yards of rope free. Use the extra rope to secure you to the belay above your position.

3 Form a loop with a figure-eight knot and secure it to the belay. The belay must be sufficiently firm to hold you and your partner should he fall.

4 Throw down the rope from the belay. Your partner ties the end around his waist using a figure-eight knot and secures the end to prevent slippage.

5 Pull in the slack and feel your partner's weight. When he begins to climb (shouting "Climbing now!" to warn you), continue to take in slack. Should he want to move downward or sideways, he shouts "More rope!" and you pay rope out to him. Hold your partner safe until he has secured himself independently to the belay.

Rope end (knotted around your waist) secures you to belay

Rope up from partner circles your waist

Rope curls around to belay

HOLDING A FALL

If your partner falls, brace your feet firmly and lean back while pulling your slack-controlling hand sharply across your body. Avoid pulling or leaning on your belay – support your partner yourself. Lower him to a point where he can start climbing again, or to the end of the rope.

Grip rope and lean backward

Pull hand over body to brake rope

TRAVERSING SNOW

SNOW AND ICE MASK THE TERRAIN and create obstacles for which special techniques and equipment may be needed. When moving over snow, ventilate or remove clothing, especially in sunshine, before you start to sweat. When you stop, replace the clothes you removed while you are still warm.

POLAR EQUIPMENT

Polar clothing must trap warming layers of air effectively, but have zippers and flaps to allow easy venting of perspiration. Outer garments must be windproof and breathable, rather than waterproof.

Hood
To prevent frostbite, the skin must be well covered. The hood should be deep enough to pull forward and shield the face from the cold wind.

Gloves
You need three kinds of glove. For fine work, the two outer pairs are removed, leaving only thin gloves to prevent skin from sticking to metal. Woolen gloves follow, then a pair of waterproof outer mittens.

Jacket
A jacket should be windproof, roomy enough for several layers of clothing, and provide good insulation.

Ice Ax
Use an ice ax for cutting steps in icy slopes and braking if you slip and fall.

Ice Hammer
This is used for hammering ice screws into solid ice for protection when climbing.

Pants
Pants or ski pants (high-waisted pants with shoulder straps) should be insulated with a windproof outer layer. Rear zippers permit natural functions without exposing too much skin.

Boots
These should consist of plastic, insulated outer shells and thick inner boots soled for use in tents and around camp. They should be worn over several layers of thin and thick socks.

MOVING ON SNOW AND ICE

It is easier to travel over snow and ice than to wade through it, but even snowshoes require skill and are very hard work. Crossing snow requires great care to avoid dangers hidden underneath. Groups should rope together, especially in crevasse country.

Mountain Skis
A mountain ski has a friction skin, a synthetic strip that is glued to the underside. The skin surface provides traction for uphill climbing, lying smooth for downhill skiing.

MOUNTAIN SKI

ADJUSTABLE POLES

Cross-country Skis
Cross-country (langlauf) skis are long and narrow, with a slightly arched profile underfoot, curving down to the tips. To move forward, your back foot pushes down on its ski to make it grip the snow, while you use the pole on your other side to push the other ski and make it glide.

CROSS-COUNTRY SKI

Molded underside of cross-country ski prevents backward sliding

CROSS-COUNTRY POLE

Crampons
Crampons are fitted to boots to increase their grip on ice. For backpacking, you need standard crampons with 8, 10, or 12 points. Forward-projecting points are for ice climbing only.

Snowshoes
The function of snowshoes is to distribute the weight of the body over a wider area of snow. Without practice, however, using them can take as much energy as using boots only.

PROTECTING YOUR EYES

Snow reflects lots of ultraviolet light upward, directly into your eyes. Glacier glasses have protective side panels and very strong filters to block the harmful ultraviolet rays, as well as reduce the level of glare entering the eyes. Snow goggles give greater protection from wind-driven snow. Eye protection must always be worn in a frozen environment.

SNOW GOGGLES

Fitted side panels ensure complete protection of the eyes from harmful ultraviolet rays

GLACIER GLASSES

CROSSING WATER

ALL WATER IS POTENTIALLY DANGEROUS, especially when it is moving. Before entering, scout a good distance to either side for a bridge or well-used fording place. Remember that, standing on a bank, you cannot see the bottom all the way across and there may be hidden hazards. Always cross with caution.

ASSESSING A CROSSING POINT

If you know what to look for, the lay of a river and the appearance of the water surface can offer clues to help you judge the safety of a crossing point. Before you cross, check the steepness of the far bank.

Standing Waves
Waves that stand still are caused by underwater rocks or strong current flow, deflecting water upward.

Covered Rocks
Rocks below the surface deflect the water above them, causing eddies.

Exposed Rocks
Exposed rocks are often slippery underfoot and the river bed may be very deep around them.

S-bend
Cross between bends. Water flows fastest on the outside of any bend.

Debris
Avoid debris, vegetation, or fallen trees that could drag you underwater.

Undercut Bank
A high bank, or one that has been scoured out and undercut, makes climbing out of even slow-moving water very difficult.

Gravel Shoal
Shoals are usually safe, but remember that the water may flow fast on the other side.

WADING ALONE

When crossing water alone, probe the bed for rocks or holes with your pole, then use it in the water as a third, supporting "leg." Place the pole upstream of you and lean on it as you lift your leading foot, sliding your foot sideways across the current and replacing it firmly.

Direction of journey

Use a stout, strong pole for support

Direction of flow

CROSSING WITH ROPES

1 Person B secures one end of a long rope (the "safety line") around a rock, then passes the other end to Person A, who is the strongest present. Person C knots a carabiner (a metal clip) into the center of a second rope (the "crossing line"), and, keeping hold of one end, he passes the other end to A. Person A crosses the river with both ropes, using a pole to probe his way safely ahead.

2 At the far bank, A secures the safety line. He clips the carabiner to it, then wraps the end of the crossing line round himself. The carabiner is pulled back, and B clips it to his belt. Person B then crosses, upstream of the safety line and holding on to it. Person C pays out the crossing line, while A pulls it in, ready to support B if he slips.

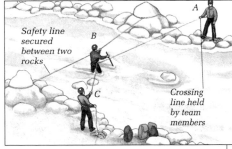

Safety line secured between two rocks

Crossing line held by team members

3 Person B unclips the carabiner, attaches it to the safety line, and C pulls it back. The backpacks are now pulled across with their carrying straps clipped securely to the carabiner. The safety line may need tightening to keep the backpacks out of the water. C unties the safety line, loops it around himself, and crosses the river. Persons A and B pull in the crossing line, ready to support C.

USING BOATS

Dᴜʀɪɴɢ ᴀ ʙᴀᴄᴋᴘᴀᴄᴋɪɴɢ ᴛʀɪᴘ in the wilderness you may need to use small watercraft, either as the pilot or as a passenger. Never be persuaded to use a boat that you believe to be inadequate or inappropriate for the task ahead, and do not entrust your life to a boatman who you suspect is incompetent.

Sᴛᴏᴡɪɴɢ ᴇᴏᴜɪᴘᴍᴇɴᴛ

Safety must be the overriding consideration when loading any boat. Distribute the equipment evenly and get everybody aboard when you finish to check that the boat is not too low in the water.

Loading Forward
The weight in the forward area can be roughly equal to the weight in the stern when moving slowly in calm, sheltered waters. If you are going to sea, or using a powerful outboard engine, reducing the weight forward allows the bow to lift easily.

Anchor
Keep the anchor ready for use, but lashed down and padded to protect the hull.

Heavy Equipment
Individual heavy items should be stowed in the middle of the boat, or toward the stern, where stability is greatest.

Loading Aft
If you are using an outboard engine, all items related to it, such as spare fuel lines, tank, and engine spares, should be conveniently close by in a waterproof box in the stern.

Painter
Keep the painter (bow rope) coiled neatly in the bow of the boat, ready for immediate use. Make sure that it is never inaccessible, tangled, or buried by luggage.

Deck Space
Keep the deck in front of passengers clear, so that their feet cannot be ensnared.

Passenger Space
Never take risks by trying to fit too many people into the boat.

Paddles
Keep paddles lashed to the sides of the boat, out of the way of any passengers and yet accessible for immediate use.

Engine
Water can enter the fuel lines and tank, stopping the engine. Before every trip, ensure that you have dry spark plugs and a maintenance kit aboard, so that you can deal effectively with any emergency.

WATERPROOFING YOUR EQUIPMENT

Your backpack contents should always be waterproofed against wet weather. When using a boat, the pack itself must also be waterproofed and made sufficiently buoyant to float.

1 Before placing items into your backpack, put them into light plastic bags. Stuff clothing into several bags.

2 Put a large, tough plastic bag inside your backpack, then place everything inside it. Try to trap air in the bag when you close the top to increase the pack's buoyancy. Empty water bottles also add buoyancy to the pack.

3 Lay your backpack on a waterproof groundsheet, poncho, or even your tent's flysheet, and fold.

5 Seal the ends of the groundsheet by twisting, then tie them tightly with cord. Two people can do this more easily than one.

4 Pull the two sides of the groundsheet tightly around the backpack and fold the edge down, aiming to get a good seal.

Twist each end securely to seal

6 Knot the two twisted ends of the groundsheet together, making the knot as tight as you can manage.

Double carrying handle makes bundle easy to grip in water

7 Using two baggage straps, strap down the two twisted ends as tightly as you can. The belts should be as long as possible, with reliable, buckle-type fastenings.

8 The ends of the straps can be knotted together to make a strong carrying handle, which you can grip if using the bundle as a float.

CYCLING

On a bicycle you can cover a lot of ground quickly, but high speed over rough ground can be dangerous, especially on a loaded bicycle. You should be capable of carrying all your equipment on your back as well as on your bicycle, because breaking a wheel could leave you a long way from assistance.

CYCLING GEAR

Layered clothes are best for cycling, allowing you to remove items when the exertion warms you and replace them when you stop and rapidly cool.

A helmet is essential for safe cycling, both on and off the road

Wear a windproof jacket, and keep a pullover handy to prevent chill during cycling breaks

Although night cycling is dangerous, in an emergency it may be necessary; a headlight can light your way

Gaiters keep pant legs out of the chain, and can prevent pants from being ripped by vegetation when you are traveling quickly

Footwear can be cross trainers, hiking boots, or special cycling boots that fit into toe cups

BICYCLE REPAIR KIT

You should know the function of each item of your repair kit and have had some practice using it. Check that everything fits your bicycle specifications.

BRAKE STRADDLE WIRE

BOTTOM BRACKET/HEADSET LOCKRING PIN TOOL

NUTS AND BOLTS

BOTTOM BRACKET ADJUSTABLE CUP PIN TOOL

ADJUSTABLE SPANNER

GREASE

FLEXISPOKE

PUNCTURE KIT

PUMP

TIRE LEVER

BRAKE CABLE

HEADSET SPANNER

GEAR CABLE

SPOKE KEY

CRANK EXTRACTOR

FREEWHEEL REMOVER

INNER TUBE

CHAIN TOOL

TRANSPORTING YOUR EQUIPMENT

How you carry your equipment while cycling depends on the kind of terrain you plan to cover. If you intend to stay on roads and tracks, you can distribute most of the weight in bags and panniers on the bicycle, since lifting and carrying the bicycle is unlikely to be necessary. Rugged terrain, however, inevitably demands a lot of dismounting and carrying of your bicycle to get around obstacles, and preventing back strain is a priority. In this case, you should choose a strong yet light model and use a backpack. The bicycle can then be carried over your shoulder. Before your trip, check that your pack is not too bulky for this exercise – if it is, your trip will be more difficult.

Using a Backpack
Carrying a backpack offers maneuverability over changing terrain, but your relatively high center of gravity reduces stability and increases the risk of a heavy fall.

Using Panniers
Loaded panniers give the bicycle a low center of gravity and stability. Front and rear panniers must balance, and the left and right panniers should be evenly weighted.

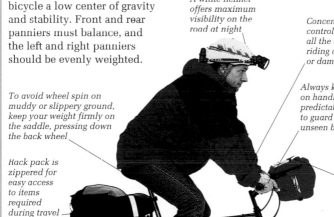

A white helmet offers maximum visibility on the road at night

Concentrate on controlling your bicycle all the time – careless riding could injure you or damage your bike

To avoid wheel spin on muddy or slippery ground, keep your weight firmly on the saddle, pressing down the back wheel

Always keep two hands on handlebars, however predictable the road, to guard against an unseen bump or bend

Rack pack is zippered for easy access to items required during travel

Transparent map case is located in top of handlebar pack

Pannier hooks over top of rack and has a second hook that fastens bottom of pannier firmly to eyelet set in bicycle frame

Chain stay is long, to allow rear pannier bag to be positioned over back axle

Low-rider front rack centers pannier over the front hub axle for optimum steerability

USING PACK ANIMALS

Do not hire pack animals without an experienced handle who understands their limitations, needs, and idiosyncrasies. Even the toughest animal may lose heart, or become resistant and immovable, if handled incorrectly. Make sure that any injuries to an animal are treated promptly.

CHOOSING A PACK ANIMAL

Local availability is the main factor in choosing pack animals. Burros and llamas carry less and travel slower than camels and horses, but they are very useful if you do not have heavy equipment.

Burros
A burro can carry 140 lb (65 kg) for 8 to 10 miles (13 to 16 km) in a day. Horses, in comparison, can carry 200 lb (90 kg) for about 31 miles (50 km). Burros travel slowly, so you must be prepared to walk at their pace.

Llamas
Llamas can keep up with a normal walking pace carrying 100 lb (45 kg) for a full trekking day. They have padded feet and have little damaging effect on pathways.

USING DOG TEAMS

Attempting to be the first to reach the South Pole, British explorer Captain Robert Scott used ponies, but they perished. A Norwegian team, led by Roald Amundsen, used dogs that survived to help Norway beat Scott to the Pole.

Traditional Transport
The traditional form of polar transport, sled dogs are still considered to be best for pulling supplies across snow and ice. Incredibly hardy, able to sleep out in blizzards and move quickly over all but icy ground (which cuts their feet), dogs are much easier to maintain than vehicles.

Steering is achieved by the driver shifting his weight from one side of the sled to the other

Sled runners are coated with hard plastic to reduce friction

USING CAMELS

Camels are able to carry around 600 lb (272 kg) over all terrains. Their long legs enable them to negotiate deep, fast-flowing rivers that would be too dangerous for humans to ford. Their large, flat feet allow them to cross sand and snow, as well as rocky ground.

Loading a Camel
Camel loading is a tricky and sometimes hazardous operation. The camel is made to kneel and a rudimentary saddle is fitted over its hump or humps. The load is carefully balanced on either side of the saddle, with additional items secured over the top. If the animal feels that the load is too heavy, it may refuse to rise, scream, spit, or even attempt to bite.

On the Trail
Camels are equally at home in hot or cold deserts, in mountains, or in sand or snow. Particularly if working hard, they should be fed and watered daily. Carrying a load, they walk steadily for up to 17 miles (27 km) per day depending on terrain, and farther on flat desert. However, camels may be adversely affected by high altitudes.

Caring for Camels
Like all pack animals, camels are far from being pets, and should not be treated as such. However, a daily inspection, incorporated into their regular daily routine, serves to identify problems before they affect the animal's health or performance. Ensure that loads are not rubbing and creating sores, that grit is not lodged under the saddle, and that insects are not biting and irritating the animal. Inspect the tack as well, to ensure that it is sound and not rubbing and causing injury.

Grooming dislodges ticks and insects

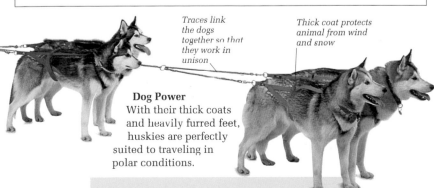

Traces link the dogs together so that they work in unison

Thick coat protects animal from wind and snow

Dog Power
With their thick coats and heavily furred feet, huskies are perfectly suited to traveling in polar conditions.

READING A MAP

A MAP CONTAINS FAR MORE information about what is on the ground than an aerial photograph. Check the map date (in the lower right-hand corner) – you may need to make allowances for recent developments. Be wary of maps of developing countries because their accuracy is very variable.

MAP SCALE

The scale of a map is given in the key at its foot, usually as a ratio of one unit of measurement on the map for a given number of such units on the ground. A good map scale for backpackers is 1:50,000, which is the metric counterpart of maps of one inch to one mile.

Houses   *House*

House   *Barn*

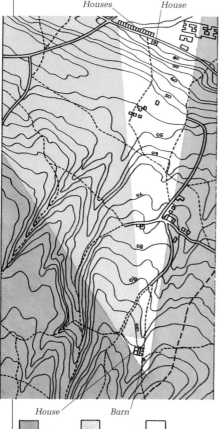

Houses   *House*

House   *Barn*

Areas out of photograph	Distant items are concealed	Distant items are visible

Comparing Map and Ground
From any vantage point on the ground, you will be able to see only parts of the countryside ahead of you. Comparison of the photograph *(above)* and map of the same area *(left)* shows how limited the view might be, and how it can be difficult to estimate the distance of objects visible on he horizon. Much map information remains hidden at ground level, especially low-lying areas that are concealed behind ridges *(see page 88)*. Holding the map, you can use compass bearings to identify the landmarks visible in front of you and work out where your route lies on the ground.

UNDERSTANDING CONTOURS

A contour line joins together places of equal height. The map key tells you the height difference between each contour. If the intervals are large, details such as gorges or cliffs may not appear.

Gradual Slope
Large contour intervals indicate a gradual slope but may conceal cliffs.

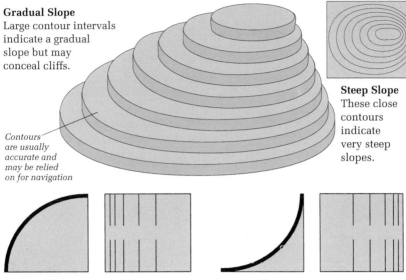

Contours are usually accurate and may be relied on for navigation

Steep Slope
These close contours indicate very steep slopes.

Convex Slope
You cannot see the top of a convex slope from the bottom, and climbers may be frustrated by meeting a succession of false summits. The contour lines are close together at the foot of the slope, and spread out toward the top.

Concave Slope
You can see the summit of a concave slope from the bottom, and at the bottom it has a gentle gradient. On a map, the contour lines of the slope bunch up together toward the top, so you can expect the climb to grow steeper as you approach the summit.

GRID REFERENCES

Most maps include a grid marked with numbers down the side (known as northings) and along the bottom (known as eastings). To make a grid reference, follow the vertical line just left of the chosen location down to the foot of the map to read its easting – for example, 04. Estimate the number of tenths from the grid line to the location – in this case, 5. Repeat with the horizontal grid line just below the location (410). Remember, "first walk into the house, then climb the stairs," and always state the easting first.

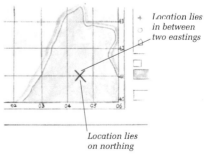

Location lies in between two eastings

Location lies on northing

Pinpointed Position
The method described above yields the six-figure grid reference of 045410. Some maps include grid reference letters for insertion before the numbers.

Continued on next page

RECOGNIZING LAND FEATURES

Many land features become instantly recognizable when you have become accustomed to interpreting maps. Hills, valleys, saddles, and ridges all have characteristic contour patterns.

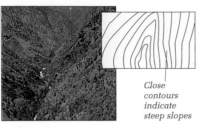

Close contours indicate steep slopes

Valley
On a map, the contours of a river valley appear as a series of V-shapes.

Hill
A hill is recognizable as a series of rings, each one a closed contour.

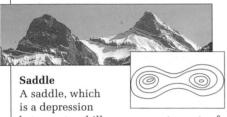

Saddle
A saddle, which is a depression between two hills, appears as two sets of circles, joined by curving contour lines.

Ridge
Ridges appear as fingers of close, parallel contours, often with closed contours indicating high peaks.

INTERVISIBILITY

Knowing which features on your map should be visible is vital in orienteering. The map *(right)* compares two sight lines, from point O to A and B. The dark sections in the profiles *(below the map)* indicate land invisible from O; the lighter areas are intervisible with O. On the map, the gray areas correspond to the profiles' dark sections.

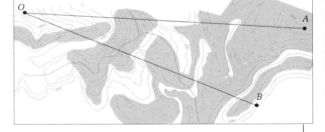

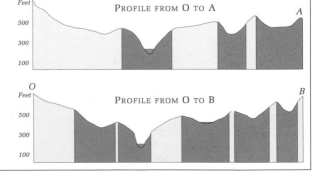

PROFILE FROM O TO A

PROFILE FROM O TO B

88

MEASURING MAP DISTANCE

Measuring map distance is vital for estimating the length of a walk and your approximate position at any time. Routes rarely follow a straight course, so your estimating technique must be flexible.

2 Rotate the paper around the pencil until it aligns with the route again. Mark the next turn in the route, noting any landmarks on the paper as you go.

1 Starting at a corner of a sheet of paper, align the edge with the route. Using a sharp pencil, mark the first turn of the route.

Mark distance from start to each easily recognized feature

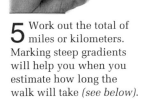

3 When you reach the corner of the paper, rotate it, continuing along the edge of the sheet. Use symbols for any features you pass.

4 When the complete route has been marked on the sheet, use the key at the foot of the map to mark each mile or kilometer on it.

5 Work out the total of miles or kilometers. Marking steep gradients will help you when you estimate how long the walk will take *(see below)*.

ESTIMATING JOURNEY TIME

When you are reading the scale of a map to determine the length of a route, remember that the distance given will be as on a flat surface, and will not take topography into account. Any estimate of the time it will take to walk a route must include allowance for time lost when climbing hills. Also, time can usually be gained when making a descent, although steep descents are likely to slow you down. A useful yardstick for estimating journey time is Naismith's Rule, which takes account of both distance and topography. Naismith suggests that you should allow 60 minutes for every 3 miles (5 km) traveled according to the map, adding 30 minutes to that total for every 985 ft (300 m) that you climb. For descent of moderate slopes, subtract 10 minutes for every 985 ft (300 m) of height that you lose, but for very steep slopes add 10 minutes for every 985 ft (300 m) of height that you lose.

USING A COMPASS

A COMPASS IS ESSENTIAL IN THE WILD – without one, it is easy to become disoriented. Remember that metal or magnetic objects may distort your readings. Any sudden, apparent change of direction should be investigated, but once you are satisfied that all is well, always "believe your compass."

THE PROTRACTOR COMPASS

The protractor (Silva-type) compass is light, very reliable, and sufficiently accurate for basic orienteering and navigation. It allows you to work out a bearing *(see page 92)* on a map, set the dial accordingly, and then use it as a direction finder, without making additional calculations.

Direction arrow points the way when compass has been set in relation to magnetic north

Bearings are read at the point where tail of direction arrow cuts dial (graduated with the 360 degrees of a circle)

Parallel lines on base of movable compass housing are aligned with the north-south grid lines on your map to orientate compass

Measurements are used for assessing journey distances while using maps drawn to different scales

MAGNETIC VARIATION

Using a compass and map may be complicated by a slight difference between the north indicated by the grid on your map (grid north) and the north shown by your compass (magnetic north). In some areas this magnetic variation is insignificant. However, in high latitudes magnetic variation increases significantly, and it can, in some places, make compasses useless. It is vital to know the magnetic variation in your area (found on your topographical map) when you are navigating and to make any necessary subtraction or addition to your bearing.

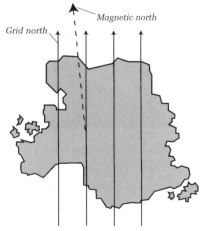

Magnetic north

Grid north

THE PRISMATIC COMPASS

A prismatic compass is more accurate than the protractor type, both for navigation and taking bearings. Its luminous dial and lockable bearing scale make it preferable for night navigation.

Sighting the Compass
When sighting with a prismatic compass, the lid is pulled upright and the eyepiece rotated into its reading position.

Luminous strip for night navigation with compass lying in open, flat position

Hinged lid has a vertical hairline that should bisect your target when sighting

Free-floating magnetic compass card

Eyepiece contains a magnifying prism

Graduated, movable outer ring

Thumb ring for holding and steadying compass has luminous notch for night navigation

Luminous strip aligns with north for night navigation

USING A PRISMATIC COMPASS

For navigation, set the compass with the magnetic bearing you wish to follow. Then, with the lid open, align the north needle with north on the dial. When walking, keep the two norths aligned.

2 Add or subtract the local magnetic-variation figure from your reading to get an accurate grid bearing. Plot the bearing on your map with a protractor and pencil, aligning zero degrees on the protractor to north.

1 With the compass pressing against your cheek, look through the eyepiece and align the hairline in the lid with the object you have chosen as a bearing marker. Looking slightly downward, read the magnetic bearing on the disk against the hairline – this is refracted to your eye by the prism in the eyepiece. The illustration *(above left)* shows the bearing (45 degrees).

3 To set a map bearing, add or subtract magnetic variation, then set the bearing on the compass. Align the north pointers to see your direction.

Continued on next page

91

SETTING YOUR COMPASS

Orienting yourself on the ground involves finding north (and the top of your map), then either turning around so that you and the map are facing north, or rotating the map to point in your direction of travel. You may then set your compass to the map.

1 To find the bearing from point A (your position) to point B (your destination), lay the compass on the map with the direction arrow pointing the way you wish to go. Read the distance between A and B using the scale on the compass edge and compare it with the map scale.

2 Without moving the compass, turn the central dial until the parallel north–south lines align with the grid lines on the map. The north (red) arrow on the dial should point to grid north *(see page 90)*. This sets the bearing (the angle lying between the line A–B and magnetic north) into the compass.

3 Turn the map until the north arrow on the compass dial aligns with magnetic north, as indicated by the needle. The direction-of-travel arrow at the end of the compass will now point to the bearing that you have set and which you will follow.

Keep north on dial aligned with north on magnetic disk

4 You can now hold the compass and follow the direction arrow. Make sure you keep the north arrow on the dial and north on the magnetic disk aligned. When following a bearing, always keep the compass level to prevent the magnetic disk from sticking and giving a false reading.

LOCATING YOUR POSITION

You can find your approximate position by choosing two or more landmarks, identifying them on the map, and orienting the map to them. Use your compass to get a more accurate fix of your position.

1 Survey the terrain and pick out two landmarks that are likely to feature on your map. These landmarks (two houses are selected here) should lie at least 20 degrees apart from your vantage point.

2 Take a bearing to the first house. Add or subtract the magnetic variation *(see page 90)* if it is large in your area; otherwise you can usually ignore that procedure. Identify the feature on your map.

3 Draw the back bearing by adding or subtracting 180 degrees from your original bearing, or by reading 180 degrees opposite your original bearing on the dial of your compass.

4 Take a bearing to the second house (which must be at least 20 degrees away from the first and easily identified on the map). In jungle, moorland, desert, or snow, there may be only hilltops, so use map contours to determine the location of each one.

5 Mark the second back bearing on the map, adding or subtracting 180 degrees as in Step 3. Your position lies where the two back bearings intersect. A third back bearing intersects as a triangle – inside which you are located.

NAVIGATION METHODS

NAVIGATION CONSISTS OF TAKING bearings and estimating distances, and it helps know some "tricks of the trade." You can confirm your direction simply by using a compass, but factors such as rough terrain, thick vegetation, and unseen obstacles can make it quite difficult to stay on course.

AIMING OFF

Following a compass bearing is only possible to an accuracy of about 10 or 20 degrees, less in rough country. If you attempted to walk directly to the fork in the river *(see right)*, you could end up at either side and not know whether to continue walking to the left or right to reach the fork. By aiming well off to one side of your compass bearing, you will have no doubt, when you reach the river, of which is the correct direction you need to take to get to the fork.

Direct route to fork in river

Turn to side to reach destination

Aim to one side of course

CONTOURING

You can waste a lot of energy when following a compass bearing involves repeatedly climbing up hills and then losing height. The technique of contouring uses the compass only as a general direction reference point, while you follow a contour line on the map, staying at the same height as you negotiate the hills and ridges between you and your objective. Contouring is particularly valuable in the jungle, where following a bearing is impractical.

Hill stands in way of compass bearing

Follow contours of hill to keep to the same height

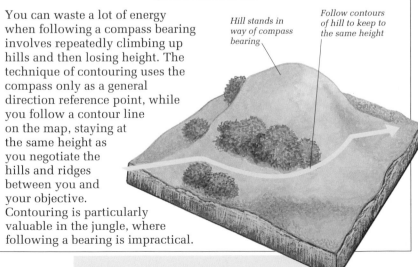

FOLLOWING A HANDRAIL

Navigation can be difficult if your destination lies behind a large feature, such as a hill, that hides your destination from view and makes it impossible to take a direct bearing onto it. Rather than attempt exact orientation with map and compass, you can aim for a linear feature on the map that will lead you (like a handrail) to your destination. Features commonly used as handrails include rivers, ridges, and roads. First, take a bearing to the handrail feature (in this case a river), then walk to it. Follow the river around until the hill appears, then turn left toward your objective. If, as in this case, the handrail does not lead directly to your destination, take a handrail that leads somewhere close, then "jump off" on a compass bearing for the remaining distance.

Summit of hill is always visible for taking bearings

"Jump off" from river to your destination

Use river as handrail to conduct you to destination

Take a bearing directly to handrail

DETOURING

As with contouring, detouring takes you off your direct compass bearing, this time to avoid a large obstacle, such as a bog, that may not be accurately marked on your map. When detouring, keep the direct bearing to your objective set on your compass, and, as you skirt around the obstacle, measure the distance you have taken away from the bearing. Once past the obstacle, return to your bearing, traversing the same distance to return you to the original line.

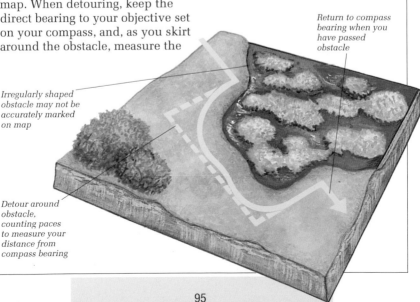

Return to compass bearing when you have passed obstacle

Irregularly shaped obstacle may not be accurately marked on map

Detour around obstacle, counting paces to measure your distance from compass bearing

CHECKING DIRECTION

KNOWING THE DIRECTION in which you are headed is the most important part of navigation. If you have no compass, it is still possible to keep track of your direction and move confidently across country, following an approximate course in relation to the sun during the day, and the stars at night.

ESTABLISHING NORTH AND SOUTH

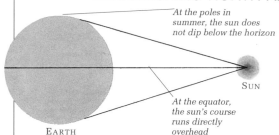

At the poles in summer, the sun does not dip below the horizon

SUN

At the equator, the sun's course runs directly overhead

EARTH

The sun rises in the east, to set in the west. After rising overhead, the sun traverses in a southerly direction in the Northern Hemisphere. For people in the Southern Hemisphere, the sun traverses to the north.

USING A WATCH

You can use a watch in conjunction with the sun to get a more accurate indication of north or south (depending upon which hemisphere you are in). You should be able to see the sun, but if it is cloudy you can get a reasonable result by aligning with the brightest area of sky.

South

Direction of sun

Northern Hemisphere
Point the hour hand at the sun. On your watch, south lies halfway between the hour hand and 12 o'clock.

North

Direction of sun

Southern Hemisphere
Point the 12 o'clock mark on the watch at the sun. North lies halfway between 12 o'clock and the hour hand.

LOCATING EAST AND WEST

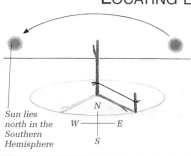

Sun lies north in the Southern Hemisphere

N
W —— E
S

Place a post vertically in the ground. To discover which direction is west, mark the tip of the post's shadow in the morning. Tie a string the same length as the shadow to a stick and draw an arc around the post. In the afternoon, mark where the shadow of the post crosses the arc: that point will be east. Then add north and south.

NAVIGATING BY THE STARS

All stars appear to move position, except for the North (or Pole) Star, which you can use in the Northern Hemisphere to find north. In the Southern Hemisphere, use the Southern Cross to find south.

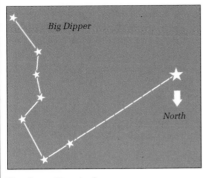

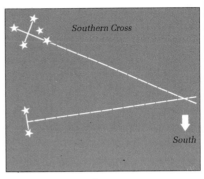

Northern Hemisphere
Draw an imaginary line between the two stars that form the front of the Big Dipper (Plough), and continue it about four times the distance between those stars to find the Pole Star. This bright star lies over north on the horizon.

Southern Hemisphere
Draw an imaginary line from the crosspiece of the Southern Cross, about four-and-a-half times its length. South should be on the horizon below this point. Two bright stars below the cross may help you find the right point.

GLOBAL POSITIONING SYSTEM

The Global Positioning System (GPS) has radically altered navigation. This system uses a collection of 24 satellites whose radio signals may be received at literally any location on Earth.

Satellite Link
Widely used in maritime navigation at all levels, GPS allows you to tune in to a worldwide network of radio signals, reflected back to Earth by satellite, to determine your position and give a clear record of your progress.

Visual display states the coordinates of your position

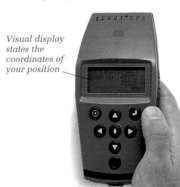

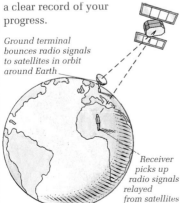

Ground terminal bounces radio signals to satellites in orbit around Earth

Receiver picks up radio signals relayed from satellites

GPS Receiver
A small GPS terminal provides constant read-outs of your position as you move. However, the GPS satellites may drop behind the horizon, creating a blank period for a short time.

FORECASTING WEATHER

WEATHER IS INFLUENCED BY TERRAIN, season, altitude, and latitude, as well as by climate. Local variations may be extreme. Modern weather forecasting depends on powerful supercomputer analysis, but there are many natural indicators that the backpacker on the ground can learn to interpret.

READING THE CLOUDS

The types of cloud overhead are determined by the temperature, pressure, and moisture content of the air in your area. Looking to windward can help you predict weather changes coming your way.

Anvil of Cumulonimbus
Tall cumulus formations develop a characteristic dark, flat-topped, anvil-shaped head that is associated with thunderstorms and heavy rain.

Cirrocumulus
Some cumulus formations do not grow. They rise and break up into tiny, high clumps resembling fish scales and known as a "mackerel sky."

Cirrostratus
High, dark streaks of ice clouds may herald rain or snow within 15 hours if accompanied by strong winds.

Altocumulus
Altocumulus are puffs and rolls of cloud, visible at medium heights. They warn of rain or snow within the next 15 hours.

Stratocumulus
Low, irregular layers of dense, gray or white clouds rarely produce more than slight drizzle or a sprinkling of snow.

Cirrus
High, wispy cirrus clouds generally indicate fair weather, but if a steady wind is blowing, they may portend snowfall or blizzards in winter.

Cumulonimbus
When cumulus darkens and begins to grow vertically, cool air is condensing moisture into droplets, making rain likely.

Altostratus
Cirrus clouds can develop into cirrostratus, and then into thicker, lower gray altostratus that may give rise to the first drops of rain.

Cumulus
Drifting, billowing puffs of white cumulus clouds against a blue sky forecast fair weather as long as they maintain their form.

Stratus
Low, shallow gray clouds produce long periods of drizzle. Cold winds can increase the precipitation.

MASSES AND FRONTS

Air masses are huge bodies of warm, cold, moist, or dry air that bring different kinds of weather as they are carried toward you by the wind. A front is formed when two air masses meet, and an approaching front brings characteristic weather changes.

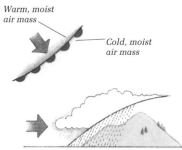

Warm, moist air mass

Cold, moist air mass

Warm Front
Warm air climbs over heavier cold air, bringing heavy rain and then showers.

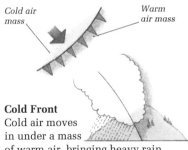

Cold air mass

Warm air mass

Cold Front
Cold air moves in under a mass of warm air, bringing heavy rain followed by intermittent showers.

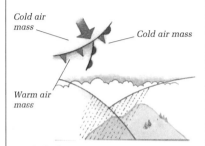

Cold air mass

Cold air mass

Warm air mass

Occluded Front
A cold front overtakes a warm front, lifting warm air above it. Rain also falls along an occluded front.

WEATHER MAPS

Meteorologists compile daily charts that plot changes in air pressure with isobars (lines joining places of equal pressure). Forecasts are made by predicting future movements of fronts between air masses with reference to regional trends.

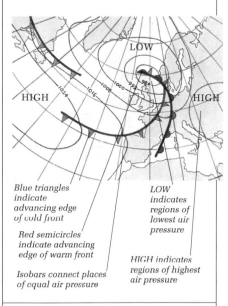

Blue triangles indicate advancing edge of cold front

Red semicircles indicate advancing edge of warm front

Isobars connect places of equal air pressure

LOW indicates regions of lowest air pressure

HIGH indicates regions of highest air pressure

NATURAL SIGNS

Some people can predict weather from visual clues and changes in how things sound and even smell.

Rainbow
A rainbow in the morning heralds showers; a rainbow late in the day signals fine weather.

Red Sky
A red or orange sunrise suggests rain or snow within a day. A red or dark orange sky in the evening indicates the approach of fine, sunny weather.

PLANNING A ROUTE

HAVING A PURPOSE AND TIME FRAME clearly in mind increases the satisfaction of backpacking. Your route should be well within the limitations imposed by the weather, terrain, and the capacity of the weakest member if you are walking in a group. When planning your route, study the map carefully and talk to walkers who know the area. Keep the need for water and campsites firmly in mind, and include enjoyable diversions such as climbing local peaks or visiting caverns or waterfalls.

1 Like any team, a backpacking group must have a leader who assumes responsibility and can assess realistically what the group can achieve. As the leader, you should be flexible in your choice of route, being ready to extend or shorten the distance, or take an easier course if some members are struggling. Even experienced backpackers feel weak and uncertain occasionally, so monitor each member and tactfully propose extra rest stops if you see the need.

2 Identify your main objectives. Marked in red on the map *(below)* is a two-day walking route. Before confirming the route, you should measure it roughly for distance and height and estimate how long it might take overall *(see page 89)*, taking into account rest periods and possible delays caused by poor weather. You also need water for the overnight stay, so plan on using the north end of the lake as the campsite (X). A revised route, incorporating the campsite, is marked in blue *(below)*.

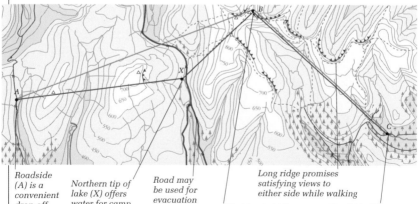

Roadside (A) is a convenient drop-off point for group's vehicle

Northern tip of lake (X) offers water for camp with minimum of deviation from original route

Road may be used for evacuation if someone is injured

Long ridge promises satisfying views to either side while walking

Climbing to high summit (B) provides ultimate motivation for trip

Roadside (C) is convenient rendezvous point with group's vehicle

3 The direct route between the starting point, the campsite, the final peak, and the finishing point is now adjusted to take account of features and obstacles that occur along the way. On the first day, the group climbs a hill, then descends to the south of the lake to cross the dam. The ridge is followed for a gradual ascent to the next summit, which is the day's main objective. Finally, the group drops down into the campsite (X), taking a safe path to the north of the line of cliffs, again using the ridgeline.

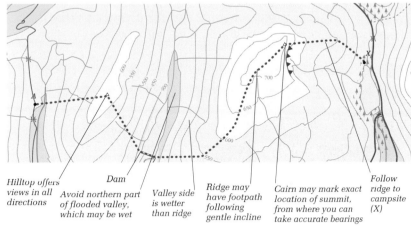

Hilltop offers views in all directions

Dam

Avoid northern part of flooded valley, which may be wet

Valley side is wetter than ridge

Ridge may have footpath following gentle incline

Cairn may mark exact location of summit, from where you can take accurate bearings

Follow ridge to campsite (X)

4 The second day starts with a diversion north to use a footpath to the initial summit, and then to the second summit (B). The group follows the high ridgeline, enjoying the views, then follows the ridge down to the road. There should, however, be a plan for bad weather while on the high ridge, because the cliffs pose a risk in poor visibility. A safety route (hatched line) is devised, contouring down from the ridge to the treeline.

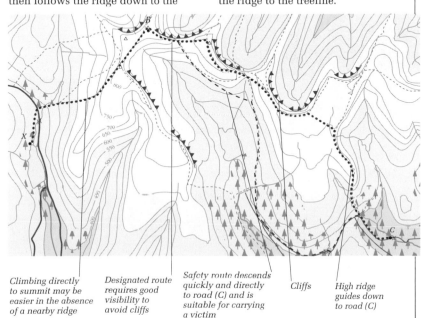

Climbing directly to summit may be easier in the absence of a nearby ridge

Designated route requires good visibility to avoid cliffs

Safety route descends quickly and directly to road (C) and is suitable for carrying a victim

Cliffs

High ridge guides down to road (C)

TAKING YOUR CAMERA

LIGHTWEIGHT, COMPACT CAMERAS solve many of the problems of backpacking photography, but they are fragile and their batteries run out. A manual-focus, semiautomatic SLR (single lens reflex) camera is more reliable. Deciding what to take depends largely on how much you are prepared to carry.

CAMERA EQUIPMENT

On the trail, take your camera cases, lens covers and hoods, and cleaning items. A flash is only necessary for interiors. A tripod can be useful. You have a choice between fixed or zoom lenses.

24 MM FIXED LENS

52 MM FIXED LENS

Lenses
A 52 mm lens gives the same magnification as the eye. Wide-angle lenses, between 18 and 35 mm, offer generous viewing angles and good depth of field. Use long-focus lenses, between 75 and 200 mm, for both close and distant subjects.

CAMERA WITH 35 MM FIXED LENS

Zoom lens has range of several fixed-focal-length lenses in one easily portable unit.

75–200 MM TELEPHOTO ZOOM LENS

Accessories
A good padded bag that holds all your equipment is ideal. Make sure you carry front and rear caps for all your lenses, plus a clear, ultraviolet filter and any other filters you normally use. For cleaning, take a blower brush and lens tissues.

LENS CAP

BLOWER BRUSH

LENS HOOD　　LIGHT AND COLOR FILTERS

PADDED CAMERA BAG

CAMERA STRAP

TAKING PHOTOGRAPHS

The best times of day to take photographs are at dawn and before dusk, when the sun lies oblique to the ground and your subjects are bathed in a diffused golden or bluish light.

Using Filters

A polarizing filter cuts down the amount of light reflected from your subject that enters the camera, with the effect of darkening bright skies, removing haze, and muting reflections from water, glass, or other reflective surfaces. The deep blue sky and the strong detail in this photograph are enhanced by using a polarizer.

Taking Portraits

A portrait is often best against a background that is meaningful or tells something about the subject's life. Even when placed out of focus, the background can still be intelligible.

Dim Lighting

Flash photography destroys atmosphere, so use natural light whenever possible. Use fast film to get a good result in dim lighting – otherwise the photograph is likely to be dark and underexposed. For a silhouette, set your light meter away from the light source.

Calculating Exposure

Light reflected by snow and ice can cause your light meter to underexpose your photograph. To prevent this, take light readings against your hand, or open your aperture one or two stops more than the aperture suggested by your meter.

Sunrises and Sunsets

The light during sunrises and sunsets changes quite rapidly. It is best to take a rapid bracket of shots each time: one at the correct light reading, one set an aperture stop above it, and one set a stop below.

4
CAMPING IN THE WILD

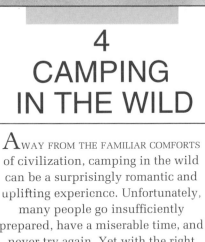

Away from the familiar comforts of civilization, camping in the wild can be a surprisingly romantic and uplifting experience. Unfortunately, many people go insufficiently prepared, have a miserable time, and never try again. Yet with the right techniques and equipment, you can be comfortable in the most extreme weather and enjoy the experience. Success begins with finding a good campsite, and the search should start early and be thorough, particularly with regard to safety.

LOCATING WATER

LOCATING WATER IS THE FIRST STEP in setting up camp, and backpackers soon become proficient at recognizing a suitable source. Ideally, water should be available for drinking, cooking, and bathing. All drinking water should be filtered and purified as a precaution against waterborne disease.

WHERE TO LOOK FOR WATER

In areas that have no surface streams, ground water is often found at the foot of cliffs, in holes below the natural water table, under dry river beds, and above the waterline on beaches.

Glaciers
Glaciers produce vigorous meltwater streams, but the water can contain abrasive rock powder, which may cause diarrhea. Before drinking, allow the water to settle, then carefully pour the separated water through a filter.

Cliffs
Look for patches of green vegetation, such as mosses or ferns, or for cracks at the bases of cliffs, from which freshwater may be trickling.

Trees
Trees indicate the presence of water.

Dunes
Dig at the lowest point between dunes until you reach wet sand. Continue to dig until freshwater seeps into the hole.

Rock Crevices
Look in crevices in rocks, where rainwater may have collected.

Dry River Bed
Digging where it appears that water used to be – for example, in the outside bend of a river – is often fruitful. Avoid the thick silt that often chokes the beds of inner bends.

Beach
Dig above the high-water mark and some freshwater will seep into the hole.

IMPROVISED WATER TREATMENT

Tripod Filter

Make a water filter by placing one thin sock inside another and lining the interior with a handkerchief or fine sand. Suspend this assembly from a tripod. Pour water into the filter and collect it in a billycan below. Purify the filtered water by boiling and/or using chemical tablets.

Salt Water

Distill pure water from salt water by boiling, collecting the steam in cloths, cooling, and wringing out the water.

TYPES OF WATERBORNE DISEASES

Anyone who becomes ill with an infection should use separate cups and utensils. Be especially careful with the person's excreta and soiled garments, which will contain the responsible organism.

WATERBORNE DISEASES		
Disease	**Causes**	**Symptoms**
Leptospirosis (Weil's disease is a severe form)	Transmitted to humans from animals Infected by *Leptospira* bacterium (rats, cattle, mice, dogs, pigs). Caught through contact with infected urine or fetal fluids. Enters through skin abrasion or lining of mouth, nose, throat, or eyes.	Causes influenza-like symptoms (fever, chills, headache, muscle pain). More severe forms lead to meningitis, jaundice, kidney failure, hemorrhage, and heart damage.
Bilharzia (schistosomiasis)	Caused by parasitic flatworm in slow-moving freshwater streams. Can enter skin directly, lodging in intestine. Also transmitted by parasites in freshwater snails.	Causes itching, hives, asthmatic attacks, enlargement of the liver, and irritation of the urinary tract.
Amoebic dysentery	Contracted by drinking water contaminated by infected sewage.	Causes diarrhea with blood and/or pus, and infection of colon. Complications of infection include hepatitis, abscess of liver and lungs, and perforation of bowel.
Hookworms	Parasite larvae enter human body in drinking water or directly through the skin.	Adult worms lodge in the intestines, causing anemia and lethargy. Larvae in the bloodstream may cause pneumonia.
Giardiasis	Caused by parasite *Giardia* in water contaminated with infected urine or feces.	Causes diarrhea and abdominal cramps. Increasingly prevalent in North America, Africa, and Asia.

CHOOSING A CAMPSITE

GOOD TIMING IS IMPORTANT when choosing a campsite – having determined the safest, most comfortable position, your tent should be up and cooking under way by nightfall. Start thinking about your campsite by mid-afternoon, and spend plenty of time in reconnaissance for possible dangers.

Collecting Water
Collect your drinking water upstream of your campsite and of places where animals drink, if possible.

Tent
Place the tent on cleared, level ground that is sheltered and well drained. Site upwind and well clear of the latrine.

Latrine
Locate this well away from the river to prevent contamination.

Fire
Position the fire close enough to the tent to smoke out insects without there being any risk of setting the tent on fire.

Washing Dishes
Clean the scraps off your plates and utensils and dry with sand or a cloth before rinsing in a bucket, because food remnants pollute the water and attract animals. Avoid using detergent since there is a risk of poisoning fish.

Washing Clothes
Saturate the clothes, then wash them on land, using soap to work up a lather. Rinse the clothes in water collected in a bucket, emptying the bucket well away from the river.

An Ideal Campsite
The tent is sheltered by trees from the area's prevailing winds, yet is not so close as to be endangered by falling dead wood. It is close to a water supply but away from animal drinking places. The site is level and well drained, and there is no danger of flooding.

Trees
While trees provide dead wood for fires or shelters, beware of falling branches that could threaten your camp.

Prevailing Winds
Looking for bent-over trees, identify the direction of prevailing winds, and erect your tent with the entrance facing away from it. You should dig your latrine downwind from your camp. Position your fire so that smoke will blow away from, not into, your tent.

River Bend
Avoid pitching your tent close to the inside bend of a river, since the land is often lower there than on the outside bend and is vulnerable to flooding. Gravel bars build up on inside bends, where the water flows slowly, and these also contribute to flooding.

AVOIDING FLOODS

Floodwaters are a hazard in mountainous areas, where a heavy storm can transform a quiet stream into a powerful, engulfing torrent in a matter of hours. Even in the driest conditions, never pitch your camp directly on a riverbed – you could fall victim to a flash flood.

USEFUL TIPS
• To prevent flooding in wet weather, dig a channel that runs around the base of your tent and drains away downhill. In high winds, keep tent guy ropes in place with large stones.
• Keep everything packed until you need it. You will know where things are, be able to move quickly in an emergency, and stand less chance of losing irreplaceable equipment.
• Never keep food inside a tent. Suspend your pack about 10 ft (3 m) above the ground, and at least 3 ft (1 m) away from tree trunks, so that animals such as bears and monkeys cannot reach it.
• Unpack your gear, do your repairs, and let your clothes and sleeping bag air in the sun for as long as possible before repacking.

SETTING UP CAMP

BEFORE YOU BEGIN A TRIP, find somewhere to erect your tent and ensure that it is serviceable. You must be able to put it up quickly in a blizzard or gale. Learn to move quickly, pegging everything down before inserting the poles and gradually adjusting the guy ropes.

ERECTING YOUR TENT

Peg corner eyelet straight and taut

1 First clear the site, removing any stones and flattening any bumps in the surface. Then lay down the inner tent with the door leeward of the wind. Immediately peg down the corners. Press in the pegs firmly, but not so hard that you bend them.

2 Lay out the pole sections in the right order and assemble them. Hook the back tent eyelet over its pole.

3 Stand the back pole upright, peg its guyline into the ground, and then repeat the procedure with the long pole, tightening the guyline until both poles stand vertical.

USEFUL TIPS

• Tie the tent guylines around large rocks if the ground is too hard or rocky to use the pegs.
• There should be an insulating layer of air between the tent and flysheet. Do not allow the two to touch or condensation may form on the inside of the inner tent, resulting in pools of water collecting on the perimeter of the floor.

Eyelet of flysheet fits over pole

4 Slip the flysheet over the tip of the short pole and peg it down at the back end only. Pull the flysheet across the top of the tent and over the tip of the long pole, and peg it down at the front, moving the inner tent's door guyline inward, toward the pole, if it obstructs the flysheet.

Tighten guylines going into pegs

5 Zip up the door flap of the flysheet over the inner tent's front guyline. This creates a covered space for storing gear. Peg the guylines around the inner tent, taking care to tighten and balance both sides equally.

Equalize tension around flysheet when pegging

6 Peg the flysheet tightly over the inner tent, making sure that it does not touch the tent walls. Unzip the front flaps and, using the guys, adjust the balance of the tent until it is tight and streamlined against the wind.

INSIDE YOUR TENT

Organize your tent so that you can reach as much as possible from inside your sleeping bag. Only unpack items as you use them, repacking when finished.

Brush tied to tent pole and used to remove snow from boots and equipment

Backpacks in porch, or left outside if space is limited

Light fixed to front tent pole with a spring clip to illuminate cooking and reading

Valuables kept safe under your pillow (a rolled pullover) where they can be checked in an emergency

Stove, utensils, water, and food laid out for use (packed away at night)

Heads of sleepers point toward door to facilitate emergency exit

Boots at end of tent (or placed inside sleeping bag to prevent them from freezing in sub-zero temperatures)

Clothing in central, area (outer edges may be prone to collected condensation)

Raingear kept to the side since they are less affected by pools of condensation than other garments

MAKING A FIRE

BEFORE STARTING TO BUILD YOUR FIRE, gather together far more ingredients than you think you might need. Everything must be dry, so in wet weather look for sheltered materials. You need a progression of sizes of fuel, ranging from the finest tinder to twigs, sticks, and branches.

FIRE INGREDIENTS

Once your kindling is lit, build up the fire by stages, gradually adding larger grades of fuel when the smaller grades have taken and are burning satisfactorily.

Tinder
Tinder is indispensable unless you are able to substitute a manufactured firelighter, such as a paraffin block.

Kindling
Kindling consists of bone-dry leaves and small sticks. Kindling is added to the fire once the tinder has taken and is ablaze.

Small Fuel
When the kindling is burning you can add sticks about the width of a finger.

Main Fuel
Large sticks act as the main fuel. They should be thicker than your finger and broken up into suitable lengths.

Large Fuel
Use thick logs to keep a fire going overnight. Ensure that they are fully burned when you extinguish the fire.

SELECTING FUELS

HOLLY

Fuels for Warmth
Soft woods, such as fir, apple, and holly, burn quickly and give off good heat. Because they burn so fast, soft woods are good for getting a fire going. However, they produce sparks, and reduce to ash rather than useful embers.

FIR

Fuels for Cooking
Dense hardwoods, such as oak, beech, birch, maple, hickory, and sycamore, burn slowly and evenly, giving off great heat. They produce coals that cook foods slowly, and each gives food its own distinctive flavor.

OAK

BEECH

Emergency Fuels
In the absence of wood, you can use fuels such as animal dung, dry lichen, moss, heather, and even blocks of peat, all of which have to be dried in the sun before use. On a seashore, dried seaweed can be used to create a good blaze.

DRIED DUNG

SEAWEED

Woods to avoid

Some resinous woods spit quite fiercely in a fire, and should be avoided when possible. These include pine and blackthorn. Other woods, such as alder, willow, poplar, and chestnut, do not burn well and merely smolder. Bamboo may explode when heated, unless split open first.

CHESTNUT   WILLOW   POPLAR

Types of tinder

Fungus
The dry, fluffy tissue inside shelf fungus makes excellent tinder. First cut away the tough outer skin of the fungus.

Dry Grass
Dry grass may be buffed into a bundle of fine fibers that easily takes a spark.

Bark
In wet weather, the inner bark of dead logs, and the sawdust produced by burrowing insects, make good tinder.

Moss
Dead, dry moss makes a fine, dense tinder. You can find moss growing on tree trunks or on boggy ground.

Dead Leaves
You can use dry leaves whole or crumbled into small pieces. Whenever you find them, save some for future use in a waterproof bag.

Preparing tinder

Store your tinder in a bag for future use

Powdering
You can trim dry sticks and bark into a powdery tinder with a knife. Make the pieces as fine as possible.

Large surface area for ignition by spark

Nicking
Cut a shallow hole in a dry fungus. A spark easily ignites the dry tissue that lies underneath.

Buffing
Materials such as dry grass may be rubbed against a stone or twisted into fine fibers of highly flammable tinder.

Continued on next page

BUILDING A FIRE

Always ensure that you have enough kindling and wood to get a blaze going quickly. A fire built in a teepee shape is efficient because the larger ingredients are dried by the gathering fire underneath.

Dig trench to a depth of 1 ft (30 cm), providing the fire with shelter from the wind

Trench Fire
A trench fire is excellent for cooking in all weathers. Having the bulk of the fire below ground level prevents it from flaring too fiercely, while allowing an adequate supply of air. A trench also helps to conserve fuel.

Star Fire
You can maintain a well-established fire by feeding four logs into the bed of embers, pushing the logs farther in as they burn. Make a star fire only in a long-term camp, where the logs will be reduced to ash before you leave.

BUILDING A TEEPEE FIRE

1 Remove a square of turf and put it to one side. Lay a platform of green sticks in the square hole.

2 Begin building a teepee shape by balancing four upright sticks against each other, their top ends meeting in a point. The teepee does not need to be very big to start a good blaze.

Opening for insertion of tinder

3 Build up the teepee gradually, trying to make it as stable and sturdy as possible – it should not collapse until it is burning fiercely. Build the teepee tall enough to create a space inside and accommodate your tinder. Also leave a space at the side through which you can introduce a match.

4 Put a generous amount of your tinder on the floor of the teepee. Strike a match and shelter the flame inside your cupped hands, allowing the flame to burn down the stem. Hold the match to the tinder until the tinder catches fire. Leave the match in place, and add more tinder, followed by leaves and twigs, taking care not to knock over the teepee.

Cup hands around match

5 As the heat builds up, the teepee catches fire and eventually collapses in on itself. This creates a hot bed of embers that can either be fed more fuel for a warming fire, or used for cooking purposes.

LIGHTING A FIRE

In dry weather, when quantities of dry tinder, twigs, and sticks are available, a match is enough to get your fire going. However, it is worth carrying another form of firelighter for use in wet weather. A firelighter that burns for several minutes has a better chance than a match of drying out wet or damp materials before igniting them.

Waterproof Matches
Scrape the wax off the match heads before striking them.

Cotton Wool
Cotton wool soaked in paraffin is a useful alternative to natural tinder.

Paraffin Blocks
These can be used to ignite large sticks if tinder is unavailable.

Fire Sticks
These sticks of treated wood shavings are very effective firelighters.

EATING OUTDOORS

Eᴀᴛ ʏᴏᴜʀ ᴍᴀɪɴ ᴍᴇᴀʟꜱ at the start and end of each day, with a substantial breakfast to get you going and a large, hot meal at night that you can fully digest while asleep. In between, nibble snacks frequently to keep up your blood sugar level, and drink plenty of water or hot beverages.

Hᴏᴛ ᴅʀɪɴᴋ

Hᴏᴛ
ᴏᴀᴛᴍᴇᴀʟ

Hᴏᴛ ᴅʀɪɴᴋ

Heating Water
Start the day by heating water and making a hot drink. When heating water on a stove, conserve fuel by using a lid on the pan and heating the water to boiling only when necessary.

Breakfast
Next, hot oatmeal, with added nuts and dried fruits, is an excellent energy source. Allow the oats time to absorb water before cooking. Fill your vacuum flask when you heat water for another hot drink after breakfast.

Cʜᴏᴄᴏʟᴀᴛᴇ ᴀɴᴅ
ᴄᴏᴏᴋɪᴇꜱ

Hᴏᴛ ᴅʀɪɴᴋ

Tʀᴀɪʟ ᴍɪx

WATER

Breaks
Eating little and often during the day maintains your energy output without you having to stop, prepare a meal, and digest it. In cold weather, always leave camp in the morning with a vacuum flask of hot water or hot drink. Do not be surprised if you feel the need for a high-calorie snack soon after hitting the trail; digesting your breakfast itself burns up energy. Add plenty of sugar to your hot drinks to make them a potent source of energy. Herbs, such as mint, impart delicious flavoring to tea.

Sᴜɢᴀʀ

Tᴇᴀ

Mɪɴᴛ

Lunch

Many backpackers designate times during their day for two "lunches," at which they stop, rest, and consume drinks and snacks. Hot soup, with added crumbled digestive biscuits for energy, is a good choice in cold weather. It is important to maintain your blood sugar level, because if you allow it to fall by walking on without taking any sustenance, you will suddenly feel weak and cold.

HOT SOUP AND BISCUITS

Dinner

Dinner should be varied and substantial. Start by soaking dehydrated foods, such as lentils for an all-in-one stew *(see page 118)*, or they will absorb water from your digestive tract and cause constipation. Use plenty of water in your cooking for the same reason. Many backpackers relax over the evening meal, leaving an hour between the soup and main course, and another hour before dessert, to enjoy the meal to the full.

Cook lentils only when soaking time is completed

SOAKING LENTILS

Soup may be a dried variety or improvised from ingredients such as stock cubes

SOUP

Enjoy peach juice before eating fruit

PEACH JUICE

Experiment with whatever ingredients you have on hand

ALL-IN-ONE STEW

PEACHES

Retiring to Bed

Drink plenty of liquids at bedtime to prevent dehydration. It is better to be woken in the early morning by a full bladder than by thirst and indigestion caused by daytime sweating and the consumption of freeze-dried foods. In cold weather, a hot, sugared drink helps keep you warm while sleeping. Before you go to bed, fill your flask with hot water so that you can make a hot drink the next morning without having to get out of your sleeping bag.

HOT DRINK

PREPARING FOOD

SAVE YOUR BEST EFFORTS for your evening meal, when you have plenty of time for preparation. Simple stews are often best, cooked with plenty of water. Adding fresh items to processed foods makes a tremendous difference, as does a little cooking oil, herbs, or spices such as curry powder. Never throw food away – eat everything you cook!

THE ALL-IN-ONE STEW

Interesting stews can be created by combining whatever food items you are carrying. Start with foods that require thorough soaking and prolonged cooking, and aim to have everything within the mixture cooked at the same time. Adding cheese or a dried meal thickens a stew to a satisfying consistency. Soak dried foods well before cooking to ensure that any large chunks are completely rehydrated.

CHEESE

STOCK CUBE

TOMATO PASTE

DRIED MEAL

BROKEN BISCUIT

ONION

PASTA

GARLIC

PEPPER

SALT

HERBS

CHILI

FLAVORINGS

Seasonings such as pepper, spices, and herbs are light to carry and transform stews and camping meals. Many backpackers are particularly fond of hot curries, carrying small amounts of ghee (clarified butter) or oil, and a variety of curry spices. You can carry fresh chili peppers, garlic, and ginger in airtight containers.

PEPPERS

NUTMEG

CINNAMON

GARLIC

DRIED MEALS

Prepare dried meals in their bags by adding hot water and resealing. They can be kept in your shirt and eaten warm on the trail.

RICE

EGG

CHICKEN CURRY

TINFOIL BAGS

COOKING FRESH FISH

Eat fish immediately on catching, or keep alive in a container or pool. Fish cook very much more quickly than meat or vegetables. Grill over an open fire to give them a pleasant smoky flavor.

1 Make a tripod by splaying out three sticks bound together at the top. Tie three green sticks, which are slow to char, onto the outside of the tripod and lay on cross-pieces to form a grill.

2 Cut out a section of turf, dig a trench, and make a teepee fire *(see page 114).*

Tripod is kept clear until blaze dies into hot embers

3 Allow the burning teepee to collapse, and keep adding fuel until you have a bed of hot embers deep enough to sustain a good cooking temperature, but not so hot that it could burn the tripod.

4 Test the cooking temperature with the back of your hand. If it is not too hot, place the tripod over the embers with the gutted fish on the center of the grill.

Turn fish when cooking begins to produce whitish juices

5 Allow the fish to cook, keeping the grill well above the embers to prevent the fish from burning. Turn the fish at least once.

NATURAL FOODS

Some plants can be added to boiling water for a nutritious and refreshing hot drink. Add eucalyptus or mint to your tea for flavoring, or make an infusion from rose hips.

EUCALYPTUS LEAVES

ROSE HIPS

SAFE CAMPING

Having identified every likely danger and selected a safe site, you must run your camp safely. A fire is probably the greatest danger because it can set the tent on fire. Ensure that your tent is well ventilated, and never cook inside the tent since a stove can give off suffocating carbon monoxide.

SAFETY PRECAUTIONS

Many accidents occur at night. People stumble from their tents to the latrine, often in bare feet, only to trip into the remains of the fire or into unseen water, or get lost or injured in the darkness.

Prepare for Danger
Good planning can prevent many common campsite accidents. When you set up camp, visualize how the camp would seem at night. Remove clutter and rope off any unsafe area.

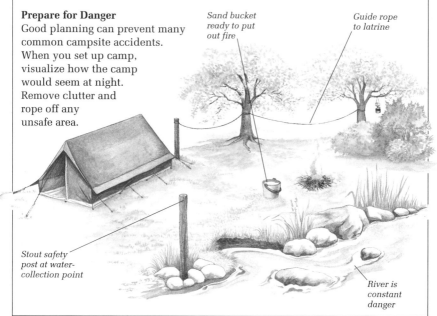

Sand bucket ready to put out fire

Guide rope to latrine

Stout safety post at water-collection point

River is constant danger

BUILDING A LATRINE

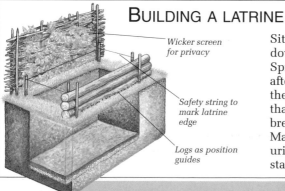

Wicker screen for privacy

Safety string to mark latrine edge

Logs as position guides

Site the latrine downwind of your tent. Sprinkle earth into it after each use, avoiding the use of chemicals that inhibit the natural breakdown of wastes. Mark a separate urination point with a stake, over to one side.

CAMPSITE PESTS

Campsites may be invaded by anything from hungry bears and curious monkeys to swarms of ants or midges. Many of these pests are attracted by the smell of food, so seal items that could act as "bait." Never encourage animals to return to you by feeding them.

Blackfly
Brush off blackflies – their powerful jaws can bite through clothing.

Ants
Look for ant nests before you pitch camp, and also for trails to water.

Mosquito
Use an insect repellent and burn a coil at night to clear your tent.

Scorpion
Shake your sleeping bag, boots, and clothes to eject possible scorpions.

Rattlesnake
Check your tent and sleeping bag to ensure that no snake is inside.

Brown Rat
Leave no food around, because rats will find it and search for more.

Brown Bear
Never feed bears. They are dangerous and may eventually cause harm.

Skunk
Skunk spray is vile. If a skunk appears, back off and keep clear.

Monkeys
Avoid playing with monkeys because their bites may be poisonous.

SAFEGUARDING YOUR FOOD

You can make food inaccessible to most insects, birds, and mammals by hanging it on a plate from a branch. Insects and birds, some of which may carry disease-causing organisms, can be kept out by enveloping the holder in a fine mesh cover that also allows the food to air. Keep food inside the holder only for the short period preceding your meal.

STRIKING CAMP

GIVE YOURSELF A DEADLINE for leaving the campsite, then work toward being totally packed up by that time. In bad weather, tents should come down last of all, after which everyone must be ready to walk out – waiting for stragglers makes a bad start to the day, especially in poor weather.

CLEARING THE CAMPSITE

Leave the campsite exactly as if you had never been there. Try not to leave the site scattered with food particles that could attract insects. Take garbage away with you, including human waste when in an environmentally sensitive location. This ensures that the wilderness remains unspoiled for future generations of visitors.

Dismantle your tent last of all and leave site immediately after your equipment is fully packed

Latrine must be filled in, returfed, and labeled with the date of your departure to inform future campers

Fire must be completely out and ashes scattered and dug well into the ground. Collect and take away unburned debris

Pack your garbage in plastic bags and take it away with you

Erasing Your Presence
Your visit should cause no deterioration of the campsite. Simply concealing garbage, for example, is not acceptable because it will be found and exposed by animals. Seeing the litter, others will clean up with less care than they would in a pristine site, and thus you will have begun a cycle of decline.

USEFUL TIP

Open your empty cans top and bottom, then burn them out in the fire to remove any scraps of food that could putrefy. Flatten the cans and insert the two cut-out ends for carrying out of the wilderness.

FLATTENED CAN

CLEANING UP THE FIRE

1 When the fire has burned down, scrape the remains into the center until they have crumbled to ash. When the ash is cold, spread it around and dig it well into the ground.

2 Making sure that there are no ashes on the surface to kill the grass, fill in the fire pit with soil. Smooth it down, then replace the turf that you originally cut to dig the fire pit.

3 Fill in the edges of the cut turf with soil and grass so that there is no visible trace of a join. Scatter leaves and grass over the site so that it is indistinguishable from the surrounding area.

DISMANTLING THE TENT

Get into the habit of striking your tent ("pulling pole") just before you move out. In very cold or wet weather, pulling pole on time prevents people from getting cold and wet while they stand around.

1 Remove all pegs securing the flysheet and inner tent, keeping hold of the tent and flysheet if there is a wind. Take special care with the pegs – never use guylines or tapes to pull them from the ground, and always count them.

2 Remove both poles, wiping the sections clean before stowing them in their bag.

3 Lift the flysheet from the tent, holding it by the pole eyelets. After checking that it is dry, fold the flysheet in half lengthwise and lay it on the ground.

5 Pack the tent bag, inserting first the clean poles and pegs in their separate bags, then the tight rolls of the flysheet and the tent.

4 Roll the flysheet tightly, folding in the sides and guylines. Then shake out the inner tent, fold it, and roll it in the same way. Check that the guylines are not tangled or knotted before tucking them in.

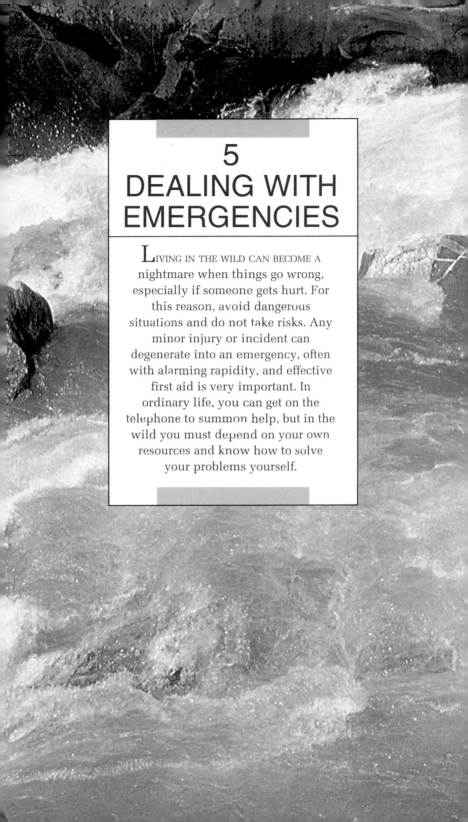

5
DEALING WITH EMERGENCIES

Living in the wild can become a nightmare when things go wrong, especially if someone gets hurt. For this reason, avoid dangerous situations and do not take risks. Any minor injury or incident can degenerate into an emergency, often with alarming rapidity, and effective first aid is very important. In ordinary life, you can get on the telephone to summon help, but in the wild you must depend on your own resources and know how to solve your problems yourself.

EXTREME WEATHER

ABNORMALITIES IN TEMPERATURE and atmospheric pressure
can bring sudden, extreme weather. Natural weather
indicators, such as the sky, give some warning, but carrying
a small transistor radio is recommended, so that you can listen
to more reliable predictions based on collected data.

WORLD WEATHER

Extreme weather is normal for some regions, while other regions experience it only rarely. Weather forecasters use synoptic charts to predict how masses of air are likely to interact. The accuracy of predictions depends mainly on the number of masses involved.

Good weather with high pressure, trapping pollution to create smog

Blizzards

Low-pressure systems, or cyclones, bring dark weather

Atlantic gales

An occluded front is indicated by spikes and humps together, where cold fronts catch up with warm ones and keep them off the ground

Squall line along which tornadoes are likely to run

Spiked lines show where fronts of heavy, cold air are pushing under lighter warm air

Weather Forecast
This idealized synoptic chart (a map on which weather is marked) shows extreme weather conditions. Once all the available information has been gathered from weather stations and meteorological satellites, and marked on the chart, likely weather conditions in the area can be forecast for up to a week.

Isobars join areas of equal air pressure

Symbol shows direction and strength of wind

High-pressure systems, called anticyclones, are stable, with good weather, clear skies, and cumulus clouds

A hurricane is indicated by an isolated isobar of warm, low-pressure air surrounded by rotating, high-speed winds

WIND STORMS

Hurricanes, tornadoes, and cyclones can hit any part of the world, but visitors to areas such as the Caribbean are well advised to find out in advance when the local hurricane season occurs.

Tornado

A tornado develops when warm, low-pressure air rises to meet high winds. This creates a swirling vortex of wind that may reach 400 mph (620 km/h). If you are outdoors, take shelter in a cave, or lie in a ditch with your arms over your head. Indoors, close doors and windows facing the tornado, and open those facing away from it. Get out of vehicles and mobile homes.

Hurricane

A hurricane is a tropical storm caused by hot air rising from the sea. If a hurricane is approaching, avoid coasts and rivers, and take shelter in a cave or deep gully. Indoors, board up windows and clear up loose objects that could cause damage when blown around. Take shelter in a cellar or under heavy, sturdy furniture.

RAIN STORMS

Sudden, very heavy rain saturates the ground, leaving floodwaters on the surface. Low-lying areas are naturally most prone to flooding, so avoid visiting them if heavy rain is imminent.

Flood

Floods are usually worst in very dry areas, where the surface of the ground is saturated immediately. Walking or driving through a flood can be extremely dangerous. Save as much drinking water as possible. Collect food, matches, and bedding, and move to high ground, or to the upper floors of a building. Unless there is any danger to the building in which you are sheltering, stay put until the flood waters drop, or until you are rescued.

Electrical Storm

When rising warm air meets colder air, static electricity is created as water droplets are violently agitated. This electricity strikes the first object it encounters as it runs to earth by the easiest route. In a storm, wear rubber-soled shoes and sit on something that will not conduct electricity. Keep away from anything tall or made of metal. Lightning strikes create huge flashes, a shock wave, and very high heat, which can harm people even when they are not actually hit.

BUILDING SHELTERS

A SHELTER PROTECTS YOU from the worst of the wind, rain, and sun. An emergency might force you to build one, or you might need additional shelters for cooking or storage. In the jungle, where you must sleep off the ground, an A-frame stretcher bed is much more comfortable than a hammock.

MAKING A TEMPERATE SHELTER

Improvised shelters are flimsy, so select the most sheltered spot you can find, perhaps building a rock wall to windward. Any available manmade materials, such as plastic sheeting, should be used.

Ridgepole should be cut 2 ft (60 cm) taller than you can reach

1 To make a lean-to shelter, first cut a long branch as a ridge pole. Measure it by reaching up as high as possible and cutting it another 2 ft (60 cm) or so above that. Use as straight a branch as you can find, avoiding dead wood that may snap. Trim off any twigs.

2 Cut two supports with Y-shaped forks to about chest height, each with an extra 1 ft (30 cm) that will be hammered into the ground. Sharpen the bottom ends to make them easier to insert, especially into hard ground.

3 Hammer both of the supports into the ground with a heavy rock until they are secure and will not fall over. Take care not to break the forks at the tops of the poles. The distance between the supports should be about 2 ft (60 cm) less than the length of the ridgepole.

Place pole centrally over supports

4 Lay the ridgepole between the two forks of the support posts, allowing equal overlap at the ends. The ridgepole must be light but resilient enough to support the finished roof and withstand heavy rain and strong winds.

5 Cut several strong branches that are long enough to lean against the ridgepole at an angle of 45 degrees to the ground. This will allow maximum rainwater runoff from the roof, and also create plenty of space inside the shelter. The branches should be no more than 8 in (20 cm) apart and should overhang the ridgepole by 4 in (10 cm).

Weave top roof sapling ends over and under ridgepole to hold it in place

6 Cut plenty of straight, sturdy saplings, leaving any leaves on them to provide cover. Weave the saplings into alternate sloping roof branches until you have created a firm, stable lattice.

Weaving whole branches into roof will strengthen structure

7 Continue to weave saplings and foliage into the roof until you are satisfied that it will provide effective shelter. When, in time, the foliage dies, add new layers, weaving them in with the old. Once the roof is finished, you may wish to make further improvements, such as placing large rocks along the back to hold down the bottom of the roof in high winds, or adding side walls. Keep your campfire a safe distance from the shelter.

USING MANMADE MATERIALS

When building a shelter, keep a lookout for manmade items capable of keeping out the rain and wind. Sheets of polyethylene, plastic bags, and baling twine are always useful. Galvanized iron sheets, wooden boxes, cardboard, and plywood can also be found. Manmade materials are usually easier to fashion into a shelter than natural items.

Continued on next page

MAKING AN A-FRAME SHELTER

In the jungle, insects and other forms of animal life can make sleeping directly on the ground inadvisable and uncomfortable. With an A-frame shelter, you form a taut, level bed from an improvised stretcher forced apart by the triangle shape of the A-frame. The bed is much kinder to your back than a hammock.

1 Cut four straight branches to the length of your height plus 1 ft (30 cm), and another three branches to the length of your height plus 4 ft(120 cm). Take two short branches and lash them to a tree in an A-shape. The tree will support your shelter.

2 Make a second, identical A-frame. Set it at a distance of about 2 ft (60 cm) longer than your height from the first A-frame.

3 Ideally, both your A-frames should be tied to trees for stability. If no trees are growing the right distance apart, you should place one of your longer branches across the top Vs of the two A-frames. This pole, sturdy but light, will act as a ridgepole to keep the second A-frame upright and will also support the roof.

4 Form a tube by tying together the ends of a groundsheet (a sheet of canvas triple-stitched for strength is even better). Make a "stretcher" by inserting the two remaining long poles and pulling them apart. Pull the stretcher over the A-frames so that it straddles them and is firmly wedged in.

5 Stretch a tarpaulin across the ridgepole to make a roof. Pull it tight and tie it to trees. The roof should keep off rain, yet allow air to circulate. A mosquito net suspended under the roof, with the sides hanging down and tucked in at night, completes the shelter.

ERECTING A HAMMOCK

Hammocks are lightweight and keep you away from nocturnal animals, insects, and waterlogged ground. To be comfortable, a hammock must be stretched as tightly as possible, so it must be strong. Even when stretched tight, it will sag when you climb in.

1 Tie the hammock to trees, making it as tight as a bowstring. The hammock should be either level or higher at the head end, tied at armpit level to allow you to get in easily.

2 Secure the ties of a mosquito net slightly above the cords of the hammock. They do not have to be far above the hammock because it will sag considerably when you climb in.

3 Next, add the roof. This is a waterproof poncho that you tie to surrounding trees and spread open over the hammock. In the absence of trees, tie the cords to rocks.

4 Enter the hammock with care, as it can easily flip over and throw you onto the ground. At night, bring down the sides of the mosquito net and tuck them under you in the hammock.

SAFEGUARDING YOUR EQUIPMENT

In the jungle, it is vital to keep your equipment away from the mud on the ground and the many marauding animals and insects. The best option is to hang items high and out of reach.

Backpack
Close all the pockets and hang your backpack on a branch before you retire at night.

Boots
Suspending your boots upside-down on sticks helps dry them and deters animals from climbing inside.

SURVIVING IN SNOW

MAINTAINING BODY HEAT IS VITAL in the snow. Put on all your clothes before you get cold, and wrap your head and neck warmly. When moving, allow air into your clothes to minimize sweating. If your limbs feel numb, massage them to increase circulation. At night, when temperatures can fall very low, a shelter is necessary for further insulation against the cold.

BASIC SNOW SHELTERS

The type of snow shelter you can build depends mainly on available materials. Sticks or branches are useful to give the structure form and stability, but it is the layers of snow that provide insulation.

Natural Hollow
A comfortable shelter can sometimes be located under the branch of a conifer, necessitating little labor on your part. Look for ways to plug any gaps, but take care not to dislodge the insulating snow settled on the branches.

Snow Cave
In an emergency, hollow out a snow bank and block up the entrance behind you with snow bricks. Poke a hole in the wall for ventilation.

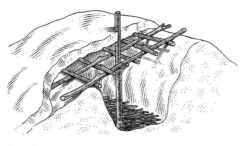

Trench
Dig a trench and make a roof by weaving some branches together. Pack snow on the frame. Remember to poke a hole through the snow so that the trench is adequately ventilated.

USEFUL TIPS

• Make at least one hole in your shelter for ventilation. Sleepers can be suffocated by their own carbon dioxide, and accumulated carbon monoxide from stoves can poison or even kill you.
• Cold air flows downhill and collects in pools, just as water does. On a sloping site, you can dig channels in the snow around your shelter and encourage descending cold air to pass by your shelter and run downhill, rather than accumulate on your floor.

BUILDING A QUINZE

Backpacks form core of shelter until it is completed

Air between snow particles will enhance recrystallization

1 Place backpacks in a tight cone to form the core of the shelter. Start collecting snow to build the quinze (pronounced "kwinzee").

2 Using a snowshoe or some other flat tool, pile snow over the packs and compact it. Wait 30 minutes for it to freeze before adding more snow.

Smooth dome to help snow harden

Insert sticks to same depth overall

3 When the snow in the pile is about 3 ft (1 m) thick all over, smooth the surface of the dome and leave it for about an hour to harden. This period allows the snow to recrystallize, bonding the particles into a hard, weatherproof shell.

4 Gather several sticks and cut them into 2 ft (60 cm) lengths. Push them into the snow all over the dome to give you a guide to the depth of the dome wall.

5 Dig down beside the quinze and burrow under the wall until you can extricate the backpacks. Then excavate inside with a hollow utensil until the sticks appear. Smooth around the dome interior until you have achieved the same wall thickness throughout.

HUNGER AND THIRST

IN ADDITION TO YOUR NORMAL food supply, you must carry 24-hour emergency rations. Routes must be planned with the collection of water in mind. You can supplement your camping food by eating wild plants, provided that you are certain of their identity, and local rules permit it.

EDIBLE PLANTS

Eating unidentified plants carries considerable risk of poisoning and an upset stomach. Examine each potential food plant carefully, taking note of its habitat and the season in which it is growing.

Summer Purslane
Leaves can be simmered in water and flavored with lemon juice.

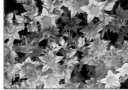

Wall Pepper
Leaves can be eaten raw or cooked as a tasty flavoring for soups.

Water Lily
Seeds, tuber, and stem are all edible, although the seeds are bitter.

Spruce
The inner bark is rich in vitamin C. The needles make a refreshing tea.

Amaranthus
Leaves and stems can be boiled in salted water and eaten like spinach.

Palms
The young shoots of some types are edible, but others are unsafe.

Almonds
Almonds are found in green husks. Discard bitter-tasting ones.

Cep
This mushroom is a delicacy, but avoid fungi unless you know them.

Wild Strawberry
Do not confuse this fruit with the deadly tropical "mock strawberry."

EDIBILITY TEST

In an emergency, you can rule out many harmful plants with these simple tests. Any plant with white sap is probably poisonous. Keep sketches in your notebook of tested plants.

1 Break open the plant and sniff. Reject any plant that smells of peaches or almonds.

2 Gently rub the sample on the inside of your elbow and check that irritation or a rash do not occur.

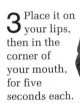

3 Place it on your lips, then in the corner of your mouth, for five seconds each.

4 For five seconds each, put the piece to the tip of your tongue, then under your tongue. If there is no burning or numbness, swallow it and wait five hours. If no adverse reaction occurs, the food is probably safe.

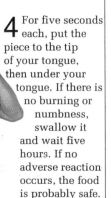

COLLECTING WATER

If you cannot find a river, stream, or waterhole, rain or dew can provide enough water for survival. Collect dew before dawn.

Dew
Wipe a cloth in wet grass to collect dew.

Rain
Collect rain in a waterproof sheet and channel it into a container. Monitor the trap in heavy rain to avoid loss.

MELTING SNOW AND ICE

In a frozen environment, snow or ice may be melted for a supply of drinking water.

Melting Snow
Hang dense, deep snow in a cloth over a container close to a fire. The snow will gradually melt. Add small pieces of ice or snow to your meltwater in a covered pan.

Melting Ice
Melt ice slowly over a tilted rock over a fire. Old sea ice, such as Arctic pack ice, is best since it contains much less salt than recently frozen sea ice.

GETTING LOST

BEING "LOST" CAN MEAN having wandered a few feet off course in thick woodland, or being several miles out of your way. Or you may believe that you had a good idea of where you are, only to be confused by inaccuracies in your map. Always stop and take stock of your position before walking on.

FINDING YOUR WAY OUT

It can be easy to get lost in flat, densely vegetated areas or in heavy mist or cloud cover, when visibility is poor. Knowing the limits of your general area makes finding your way a lot simpler.

1 Use your map to establish boundaries in the surrounding area that will be immediately recognizable if you cross them. Here *(see map, left),* you are in a basin with a road to the west and rising ground with streams to the north and south. Provided that you do not cross the boundaries, you know that you are lost only within this small, well-defined area.

2 Follow a compass bearing aimed at where you think the nearest recognizable boundary is likely to be located. Should you become confused, use the compass to retrace your steps and choose another bearing.

THE SPIRAL SEARCH

A spiral search is used to pinpoint a pathway or feature after arriving at an approximate position, perhaps after following a compass bearing. Setting the compass to one of the four compass points, walk to a point no farther than the limit of visibility, counting your paces. If the feature is not found, turn 90 degrees to the right and walk on for up to twice the distance. Continue, adding the distance of the first leg each time you turn. In time, the widening spiral will take you to your objective, with little risk of your missing it.

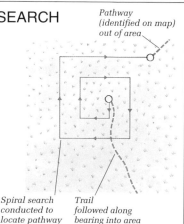

Pathway (identified on map) out of area

Spiral search conducted to locate pathway

Trail followed along bearing into area

MAKING A MAP

If you are lost, making a map enables you to collect and chart information that will be helpful in relocating your position. You can also use this kind of chart to clarify inaccuracies in your map.

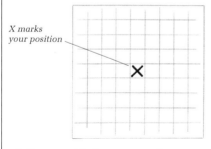

X marks your position

1 Draw a grid of squares, each one representing ¼ sq mile (0.5 sq km). Place an X in the approximate center of the map to represent your position.

2 Move to a vantage point (climb a tree if necessary) from where you can see at least three prominent features, preferably lying in different directions. Take a bearing *(see page 91)* to one feature and estimate its distance from you *(see below)*.

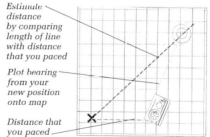

Bearing

Magnetic north

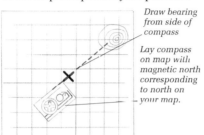

Draw bearing from side of compass

Lay compass on map with magnetic north corresponding to north on your map.

Any movement you make can be plotted in relation to map features

Intersection of lines on map gives your exact position

3 Draw the bearing you have taken on your map, lining up the grid so that north is at the top. Add the hill at the distance that you estimated.

4 Take bearings to two other features and mark them on the map. The point at which the three bearings intersect confirms your position.

ESTIMATING THE DISTANCE

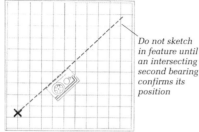

Do not sketch in feature until an intersecting second bearing confirms its position

1 Estimation of distances depends on the accurate plotting onto your map of distances that you have actually paced. First take a bearing to a feature and draw the bearing from the cross that represents your position.

2 Walk on a bearing of 45 degrees from the first bearing, counting paces, until the hill bearing has changed by 30 degrees. Plot your position, then the bearing to the hill.

Estimate distance by comparing length of line with distance that you paced

Plot bearing from your new position onto map

Distance that you paced

SIGNALING FOR HELP

LEAVE DETAILS OF YOUR TRIP with at least one person before you depart so that a search can be instigated should you fail to appear at your final destination. Knowing how to attract the attention of air-rescue teams makes their job easier and could save a life, especially if someone is injured and unable to move.

USING SMOKE

Smoke from a pinpoint source rarely occurs naturally and is therefore a reliable indication of a human presence. Fires or flares are easily seen from the air and could trigger an investigation.

Creating Smoke
On a still day, you can send puffs of smoke into the air to pinpoint your locality. Mostly, however, drifting smoke provides only a broad signal.

Using Flares
Save your flares for when you can see an aircraft, then light them in the highest, most exposed place you can find. Tying a flare to a long pole may make it more visible from the air.

GROUND MARKERS

If you have attracted an aircraft's attention, employ international, clearly understood ground signals to send basic messages. Only use the signals in a serious emergency because pilots will respond and put themselves and their aircraft at risk, especially if they see the signal "I" for serious injury.

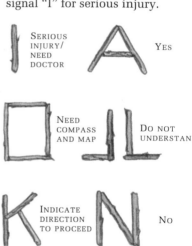

I — SERIOUS INJURY/ NEED DOCTOR

A — YES

☐ — NEED COMPASS AND MAP

JL — DO NOT UNDERSTAND

K — INDICATE DIRECTION TO PROCEED

N — NO

↑ — AM GOING THIS WAY

LL — ALL IS WELL

F — NEED FOOD AND WATER

△ — BELIEVED SAFE TO LAND HERE

USING THE SUN

A small, hand-held mirror can be used to reflect the sun and attract attention. The flash of the sun is visible for several miles, particularly from the air.

WARNING

Even weak sunlight can produce a bright beam from a heliograph, and the focused glare can temporarily blind a vehicle driver or an aircraft pilot. A heliograph should only be used in an emergency. Flash the sun's reflection to and fro over the vehicle's windscreen or the aircraft's cockpit, rather than focusing continually onto it.

Heliograph
A heliograph is a reflective surface with an eyehole in the center. Many backpacker's survival kits include one. Point it at the sun, then flash the reflection onto the ground. Move the reflection over the ground, then over to the target. By looking at the target through the central hole, you can direct the flash more accurately onto it.

SIGNALING TO HELICOPTERS

Direct helicopters to land on level, firm ground, away from vegetation, pylons, or loose items on the ground that could be sucked up by the rotor blades. Remove headgear and stand well braced against the downwash, with one foot forward, ready to turn away.

HOVER/NEED
MECHANICAL
HELP

DESCEND

(WAVING RIGHT ARM)
MOVE TO MY LEFT

(WAVING LEFT ARM)
MOVE TO MY RIGHT

FLY
TOWARD ME

FLY TOWARD
ME/PICK ME UP

Continued on next page

SEMAPHORE

When using semaphore, have someone with binoculars by your side, ready to draw the arm positions of the distant individual – the positions can be "deciphered" into an intelligible message when transmission is complete. Leave plenty of time between letters when sending semaphore messages because they are much harder to receive than to send.

A B C

G H I J

N O P Q

T U V W

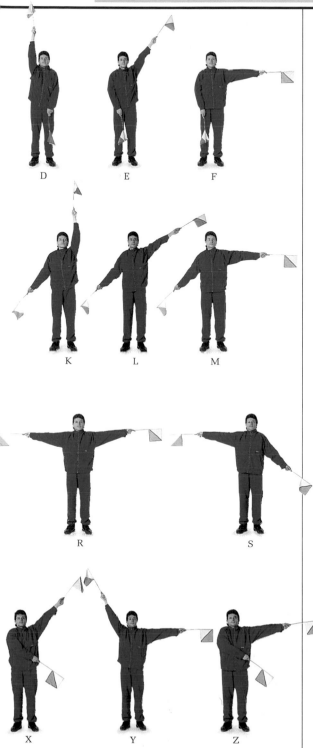

D   E   F

K   L   M

R   S

X   Y   Z

MORSE CODE

Experienced operators transmit Morse code at the same rate as they receive it, so tap out each letter slowly. Note the dots and dashes as you receive them, rather than attempting to decode them simultaneously.

A	•−
B	−•••
C	−•−•
D	−••
E	•
F	••−•
G	−−•
H	••••
I	••
J	•−−−
K	−•−
L	•−••
M	−−
N	−•
O	−−−
P	•−−•
Q	−−•−
R	•−•
S	•••
T	−
U	••−
V	•••−
W	•−−
X	−••−
Y	−•−−
Z	−−••
1	•−−−−
2	••−−−
3	•••−−
4	••••−
5	•••••
6	−••••
7	−−•••
8	−−−••
9	−−−−•
0	−−−−−
SOS	•••−−−•••

DANGEROUS ANIMALS

WILD ANIMALS USUALLY AVOID humans, but they can become aggressive if they, their young, or their territory are threatened. Do not pet or approach animals, and do not offer food. Monkeys, in particular, must be discouraged; they steal anything, and their bites may be poisonous. Even farm animals may bite or kick, and they could infect you with rabies.

Animal Hazards
Before your trip, find out which of the creatures in your destination country are dangerous. Antidotes are available for some poisonous bites.

NORTH AMERICA

Grizzly Bear
The smell of food may attract grizzly bears to your camp.

Large predators, such as the grizzly bear, the mountain lion, and the timber wolf, are flourishing in some northern forests and national parks. Warmer regions are inhabited by smaller, venomous creatures such as the copperhead snake, several species of coral snake, and the brown recluse spider.

Alligator
Alligators lie immobile for hours, then seize their prey with alarming rapidity.

SOUTH AMERICA

The large tropical rainforest area of South America contains many venomous insects and snakes. The poison arrow tree frog secretes a substance so toxic that only a small amount on human skin can kill. Larger animals, such as wild pigs and jaguars, are also dangerous to humans. On the southernmost tip of the continent, the bull elephant seal can be very aggressive during its rutting season.

Piranha
Schools of piranha kill and strip their prey clean with razor-sharp teeth.

Poison Arrow Treefrog
This frog's skin secretes a highly toxic substance.

EUROPE

Dangerous animals are now rare in Europe. The adder is Europe's only venomous snake, but its bite, like the stings of the hornet, the bee, and the wasp, is lethal only if the poison causes allergic (anaphylactic) shock. A bite from a black widow spider, found around the Mediterranean, can kill in the same way.

Hornet
A hornet's sting can trigger allergic shock.

Black Widow Spider
This spider's bite causes painful muscle spasms.

AFRICA

Africa has many large animals capable of inflicting harm, ranging from predatory big cats to the hippopotamus, which becomes ferocious when it cannot retreat or when defending its young. There are also snakes with fatal bites, such as the black mamba, puff adder, and boomslang. Mosquito-borne malaria, however, is the most significant threat to the traveler.

Puff Adder
The long fangs of this snake can penetrate clothing.

African Bullfrog
While not poisonous, the bullfrog's bite is painful.

ASIA

Cobra
Some cobras can spit venom from a distance.

In Asia, creatures dangerous to humans tend to inhabit the tropical forests of the southeast, where man is represented only by scattered indigenous tribes. Examples include the estuarine crocodile; snakes such as the Indian krait and the cobra; and the red-back spider, which is a relative of the poisonous European black widow spider.

Tiger
Jungle hikers in Southeast Asia could meet this formidable predator.

AUSTRALIA

Funnel Web Spider
This spider has a fatal bite. It is most active at night.

Australia has some of the most poisonous and aggressive creatures in the world, most of them living in the desert interior or in the surrounding seas. A bite from the fierce snake or a desert scorpion's sting can kill within hours. On the coast, the stonefish and the death pufferfish are poisonous.

Desert Scorpion
The deadly sting of a desert scorpion lashes forward on the arching tail.

AVOIDING CONFLICT

COMMUNICATING WITH LOCAL people is always preferable to being solely a spectator, but not knowing an area's language or customs can occasionally cause inadvertent offence, as well as expose you to exploitation. Being sensitive to local feelings goes a long way in avoiding awkward situations.

WOMEN TRAVELERS

Although sexual discrimination should never occur, it does, and usually against women. In places where women are sheltered or hidden from their menfolk, some individuals may be too attentive to foreign visitors; others may feel antagonized. It is sensible to wear practical clothing *(below)* that does not arouse unwanted interest.

USEFUL TIPS

• Dress modestly, in accordance with local customs, noting the body areas that local women keep covered.
• Avoid making eye contact with men, who may take this as encouragement. Wearing dark glasses helps to prevent inadvertent eye contact.
• Do not allow yourself to be seduced, either by local men or by foreigners you do not know.
• In a sexually repressed society, it may be expedient to seem totally aloof in the street, to avoid being judged "loose" and losing respect.
• In some countries, men simply do not speak to women, or take instructions from them. You have to earn their respect and get them to accept you as an "honorary man."

CULTURAL DIFFERENCES

When traveling, observe how men and women of the locality respond to each other. Imitate their manners and greeting gestures, but do it carefully and sincerely, so that people will be certain that you are genuinely trying to fit in.

Gestures
Gestures do not always have the same meanings worldwide, so use them with caution. The shrug that expresses a failure to understand is universal, but other gestures that you consider harmless may be thought offensive or even obscene.

Eye Contact
In most Western countries, people maintain eye contact for much of the time when making conversation with strangers. However, attempts to maintain eye contact may be interpreted as aggressive and disrespectful in some other parts of the world.

PHOTOGRAPHY

Overzealous photographers can cause resentment, mainly when photographing people. Always ask permission to take portraits, but decide whether you want to pay to do so if asked. Some cultures believe that you take part of their soul with the picture, so show sensitivity.

Arousing Curiosity
Photographers often arouse intense interest, so expect attention. Allow people to hold your camera and look through the lens, but always keep hold of the strap. When everyone has had a try, having you photograph them should seem more acceptable.

Causing Provocation
Taking certain pictures can get you into serious trouble. Women, or their men, may be resentful, and you may be suspected of espionage if you take photographs of factories, airfields, bridges, or government buildings. Before taking such a picture, weigh up whether it is really worth the risk.

EMBASSIES

Embassies are located in capital cities, and there may also be consulates in provincial cities. They are not there solely to help travelers, although if you are in trouble or need advice they are the places to go. If your country does not have an embassy where you are traveling, then it will certainly have an arrangement for travelers to be helped by another country's embassy. Although an embassy can lend you money to get home, visit you in prison, or forward money from home, do not have unrealistic expectations that embassy staff can solve all your problems. You will always be bound by local laws and judicial procedures, and be reliant on local hospitals for medical treatment. In the event of a medical evacuation, an embassy can arrange and finance it for you, but eventually you will be asked to reimburse the costs – another reason to get adequate medical insurance.

Representing the Nation
An embassy represents the best face of its country, with smartly dressed staff who speak the local language and strive toward good relations with the host country. Your reception there will be warmest if you dress neatly.

FIRST-AID TECHNIQUES

A MEDICAL EMERGENCY CAN OCCUR with devastating suddenness, and nowhere more so than in the wilderness, where professional help may be far away. If you are venturing out alone, you should carry a first-aid kit for the treatment of minor injuries. However, in the event of a serious medical emergency, such as hypothermia or a bad fall that results in shock or breathing failure, there is no substitute for medical know-how and advanced medical aid must be sought as soon as possible. The following pages describe the safest first-aid responses to a range of problems, from blisters to severe bleeding, but first aid is a practical skill and your confidence and effectiveness will be greatly enhanced by expert training. Many organizations offer regular courses in first aid, and every member of a backpacking expedition should complete a first-aid course before departure.

THE ABC OF RESUSCITATION

If a victim is unconscious, you must assess whether his heart and lungs are functioning. ABC, which stands for Airway, Breathing, and Circulation, is a reminder of the three steps you should take during assessment. If you suspect a back or neck injury, be careful not to move the victim's head and immobilize it as soon as possible.

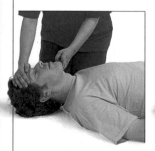

1 Open the victim's mouth and remove any obstruction. Then open the **Airway**, using the head-tilt/chin-lift technique; place the palm of one hand on the person's forehead and two fingers of your other hand under the person's chin; tilt the head back.

2 To detect **Breathing**, place your cheek next to the victim's mouth and nose for five seconds. Feel for exhaled breath against your cheek. Watch for movements of the chest to indicate inhalation and exhalation of the victim's lungs.

3 Check **Circulation** by feeling for a pulse at the side of the windpipe for five seconds. If pulse and breathing are found, put him in the recovery position *(see page 147)*. If breathing is absent, begin respiration *(see page 147)*. If both are absent, begin CPR *(see page 148)*.

THE RECOVERY POSITION

Any unconscious victim is safest lying in the recovery position. The tongue does not block the throat and liquids drain freely from the mouth, reducing the risk of the stomach contents being inhaled.

1 If the victim is unconscious but breathing, bend his near arm up at a right angle to his body. Hold the back of his far hand to his near cheek. With his nearer leg straight, bend the other knee to a right angle. Then pull on the thigh toward you, rolling the victim onto his side.

Grasping knee gives leverage for turning victim onto his side

2 Lower the victims's head to the ground, tilt the head back, and pull the jaw forward to open the airway. If necessary, place his hand under his head.

Tilt head back so that victim will not choke on vomit

Bent arm gives stable support

Bent leg prevents victim from rolling forward

ARTIFICIAL RESPIRATION

The air that you exhale contains 16 percent oxygen, which you can introduce into the circulation of a victim by blowing it into his lungs. If the victim has stopped breathing but still has a pulse, give 10 breaths a minute until the victim is breathing unaided.

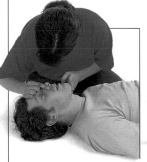

1 The victim should be laid on his back on a firm surface. To ensure an open airway, clear any obstruction from his mouth. Place one hand on his forehead, pinching his nose, and one hand under his chin, and gently tilt back his head.

2 Keeping his nose pinched shut with your index finger and thumb, seal your mouth over the victim's mouth, and blow steadily into his lungs for two seconds. Remove your mouth and let his chest fully deflate.

3 Repeat Step 2, giving 10 breaths per minute. Continue artificial respiration until help arrives or until the victim is breathing by himself. Check for a pulse. If the pulse stops, commence CPR *(see page 148)*.

CARDIOPULMONARY RESUSCITATION

Cardiopulmonary resuscitation (CPR) provides an artificial blood circulation and ventilates the lungs. CPR consists of chest compressions to maintain the circulation of blood to the brain, and artificial respiration *(see page 147)* to oxygenate the blood.

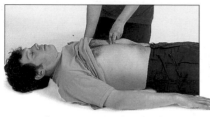

1 Lay the victim on a firm surface. Find one of his lowest ribs with your index and middle fingers, then slide upward until your middle finger lies where the rib meets the breastbone.

2 Your index finger now lies on the breastbone. Slide the heel of your other hand down the breastbone until it touches your index finger. This is where you should apply the pressure.

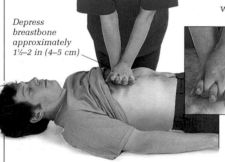

Depress breastbone approximately 1½–2 in (4–5 cm)

3 Place one hand over the other, locking the fingers *(inset, left)*. Lean over the victim with your arms straight, press down vertically, then release, without removing your hands. Do this 15 times, then give two breaths of artificial respiration *(see page 147)*.

SHOCK

Shock is a dangerous reduction of blood flow around the body that may result in insufficient oxygen and nutrients reaching the tissues. Without swift treatment, the vital organs can fail, resulting in death.

Raising the legs improves blood supply to vital organs

Take pulse at radial artery, just below base of thumb

2 Insulate the victim both above and underneath with a sleeping bag or warm coat. Check his breathing and pulse rate, particularly if he falls unconscious. Perform cardiopulmonary resuscitation *(see above)* if his breathing and heart stop. Seek help.

1 Raise the victim's feet higher than his head to help him remain conscious. Loosen his clothing, reassure him, and take his pulse.

Burns and scalds

Accidents with camping stoves, fires, and boiling water are the most common causes of burns and scalds in the wild. Prompt action prevents further tissue damage, so always treat burns or scalds at once to stop the burning, relieve pain and swelling, and minimize the risk of infection. Do not remove anything stuck to the burn.

1 Flood the injured part with cold water for at least 10 minutes to stop the burning and relieve the pain. If you are not carrying much water, plunge the injured area into a stream.

2 It is important to protect the area of injured tissue from infection. A plastic bag can be used temporarily, but make sure that the plastic does not touch the wound.

3 As soon as possible, lay a pad of clean gauze over the injured area and secure it with a bandage, but not too tightly. Do not use adhesive dressing or strapping, or apply lotions, ointments, creams, or fats (such as butter) to the affected area. If blisters have formed, do not press or pick at them because they protect the skin underneath from infection.

Use dry, nonadherent dressing, and bind well beyond the edges of the injured area

Dressing keeps out airborne germs

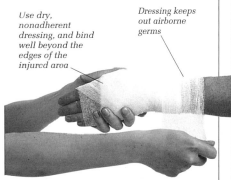

Sunburn

Sunburn, which causes redness, itching, tenderness, and blistering, results from overexposure of the skin to direct sunlight. Sunburn may be caused by "skyshine" at high altitude, even on dull days, and the reflection of sunlight by water or snow increases the risk.

1 Before treatment, immediately move the victim out of the sun into a cool, shaded place. Then, using a soft cloth, gently cool the reddened skin with cold water.

2 Give the victim water to sip, and continue to cool the skin with cold water. Calamine or an after-sun preparation may help to soothe mild burns.

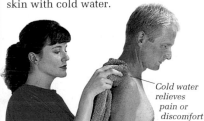

Cold water relieves pain or discomfort

HEAT EXHAUSTION

Headache, dizziness, confusion, nausea, cramps, a rapid pulse, and rapid breathing all indicate heat exhaustion. The condition is caused by loss of salt and water from the body through excessive sweating, and is common in people who have not acclimatized to strenuous physical activity in a hot, humid environment.

Support victim while he sips water

1 Move the victim to a cool place. Help him to sip plenty of water or electrolyte solution to replace the lost fluids. If the victim becomes unconscious, place him in the recovery position (see page 146).

2 When the victim has sipped a good quantity of water, allow him to rest. Raise his legs to improve blood circulation to his brain, and leave more solution close at hand.

Water is easily accessible to victim

Raising legs improves circulation to all vital organs

HEATSTROKE

The "thermostat" in the brain can fail in extreme heat, resulting in a blood temperature above 104°F (40°C). Symptoms of heatstroke include headache, dizziness, hot and flushed skin, a fast pulse, and unconsciousness. Heatstroke may occur quite suddenly.

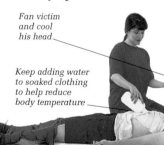

Fan victim and cool his head

Keep adding water to soaked clothing to help reduce body temperature

2 When the victim's temperature falls to a safe level (100.4°F/38°C), remove the wet material and dry him to prevent chill. Continue fanning to keep him cool. Replace the wet clothing only if his temperature starts to rise again.

1 Your first priority is to reduce the body temperature of the victim as quickly as possible. Move him into a shady, cool place, remove all his outer clothing, and lay him down. Cover the victim in cold, soaked clothing or a wet sleeping bag liner, and keep the materials soaking wet. If the person becomes unconscious, assess whether resuscitation is required (see page 146).

HYPOTHERMIA

Hypothermia is a dangerous fall in body temperature to below 95°F (35°C). Treatment should aim to restore normal body temperature as rapidly as possible. Take the victim to shelter, replace all wet clothing with warm, dry, garments, and help him into a sleeping bag. If shelter is unavailable, remove only wet outer garments and replace them with warm, dry ones. Provide a warm, highly sugared drink if you can and help him to sip it slowly to raise his body temperature.

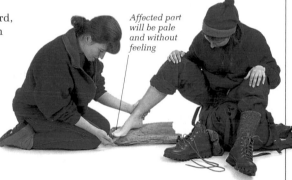

Get victim into sleeping bag as your first priority

Help victim by pulling his hand through sleeve

FROSTBITE

Exposure to frozen conditions can cause the tissues of the extremities to freeze. Minor cases of "frostnip" recover well, but severe frostbite can cause permanent damage or loss of affected tissue.

1 A frostbitten hand or foot will be numb, hard, and stiff. Take the victim to a warm place where thawing of the affected part may be attempted safely, without risk of refreezing or trauma. Very carefully remove boots and socks and evaluate the injury.

Affected part will be pale and without feeling

WARNING

• If hypothermia accompanies frostbite, treat the hypothermia first *(see above).*
• If possible, do not walk on a frostbitten foot after it has been rewarmed.
• Treat any blisters *(see page 153).*
• Do not rub the affected part, or apply hot objects that could burn the tissue while feeling is absent.

2 Warm the part between your hands or in your lap. A hand may be warmed in the victim's armpit; a foot may be warmed in the rescuer's armpit.

3 If color does not return to the part, place it in lukewarm water. Dry it carefully and apply a light dressing, bandaged without pressure.

SEVERE EXTERNAL BLEEDING

Although severe bleeding is frightening and dramatic, do not allow the bleeding to distract you from performing the ABC of resuscitation *(see page 146)*. Bleeding can usually be controlled by direct or indirect pressure and elevation of the affected part. Treatment should aim to control the bleeding and minimize the risk of infection. Allow also for the possibility of shock *(see page 148)*.

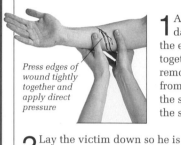

Press edges of wound tightly together and apply direct pressure

1 After uncovering the damaged area, press the edges of the wound together. If you cannot remove a foreign body from the wound, press the skin tightly up to the sides of the object.

WARNING

Internal bleeding is very serious. Although blood may not be lost from the body, it is lost from the circulation and shock will develop. If blood accumulates, it can exert pressure on organs such as the lungs or brain. Seek medical attention.

2 Lay the victim down so he is comfortable. Check for signs of broken bones in the affected limb, then raise the limb above the level of the victim's heart. Place a gauze pad or a clean dressing over the wound and apply pressure with your fingers or palm to stop the bleeding.

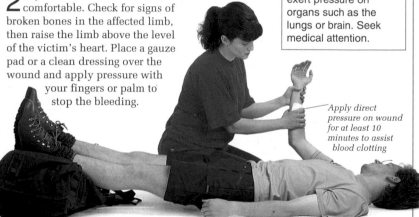

Apply direct pressure on wound for at least 10 minutes to assist blood clotting

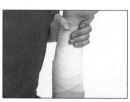

3 Apply a sterile dressing (or clean material if dressings are unavailable) to the wound. Keep the arm elevated while it is being bandaged. If you have no material, exert pressure on the wound with your hands until bleeding ceases. Cover the wound.

4 Bandage firmly, but not so tightly as to impede circulation. If blood seeps through the bandage, secure another pad and bandage over it. Build up pads on either side of any foreign body until the wound can be bandaged over without being pressed.

5 To ensure that the bandage is not too tight and is not constricting blood circulation, check the fingers or toes below the bandage for color and feeling. If the extremity is pale or feels numb to the victim, the bandage must be loosened.

SPRAINED ANKLE

Unlike a broken ankle, which involves fracture of at least one bone, a sprained ankle is a soft-tissue injury that may be readily treated. The pain of the injury is increased by movement or by putting weight on the foot. Severe swelling of the ankle is common.

1 Sprained ligaments, strained muscles, and deep bruising are all initially treated by the "RICE" procedure – Rest of the injured part, Ice or a cold compress on the injured part, Compression of the injury, and Elevation of the injured part. Directly after the injury, rest the injured part, steadying and supporting it comfortably.

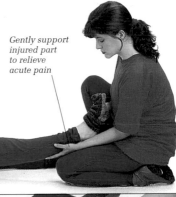

Gently support injured part to relieve acute pain

2 If ice is available, wrap it in a cloth and apply it to the injured part. If you have no ice, apply a cloth that has been thoroughly soaked in cold water.

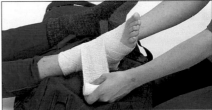

3 Apply a thick, padded bandage to compress the swelling. Elevate the injured limb on a firm support. Check the circulation every 10 minutes.

BLISTERS

Blisters should be left intact because bursting them increases the risk of infection of the underlying tissue. The blisters should be cleaned and firmly padded to prevent boots from pressing against them and causing them to burst or become larger.

1 Thoroughly clean the area around the blister with sterile water. This reduces the risk of infection should the blister burst after being dressed.

2 Gently dry the area, taking care not to burst the blister (but lift away skin if the blister has already burst). Tape a large, clean dressing over the blister. Try to prevent the boot from rubbing directly against the blister.

Strong tape is needed to prevent dressing from being rubbed off

FOREIGN BODY IN THE EYE

Anything floating freely on the white of the eye is generally easy to remove. Never try to remove a foreign body that adheres to the eye, penetrates the eyeball, or rests on the colored part of the eye.

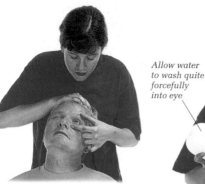

Allow water to wash quite forcefully into eye

2 If you can see the foreign body, wash it out with clean water from your water bottle or a cup. If this is not successful, and the object is not embedded in the eye, try lifting it off with a moist swab, or the dampened corner of a tissue or clean handkerchief. Avoid pressing on the object and driving it into the surface of the eye.

1 Advise the victim not to rub his eye. Sit him down facing the light, and gently separate the eyelids with your finger and thumb. Examine every part of the eye.

EYE INJURY

The eye can be cut or bruised by direct blows or by sharp, chipped fragments of grit or glass. The affected eye will cause great pain, with either a visible wound or a bloodshot appearance; a flattened eyeball may be punctured. Vision is very likely to be impaired.

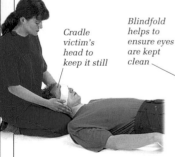

Cradle victim's head to keep it still

Blindfold helps to ensure eyes are kept clean

1 Lay the victim on his back, keeping his head still. Tell him to keep his eyes still, because movement could worsen the damaged eye. Place a gauze pad lightly, without pressure, over the damaged eye to protect it.

2 Bandage across both eyes to keep the pad in place and to prevent dirt or blood from entering the undamaged eye. Gently reassure the victim before applying the bandage.

 WARNING

All eye injuries are potentially serious. Even superficial grazes to the surface (cornea) of the eye can lead to scarring or infection, with possible deterioration of vision. A penetrating wound may rupture the eyeball and allow its clear liquid (the humor) to escape. This type of injury is very serious, although it is now possible to repair the wound and save the victim's sight.

OBJECT IN THE EAR

An object blocking the ear canal can cause temporary deafness; insects trapped in the canal cause alarm as they buzz or move around. Warm oil will immobilize an insect, but the safest way to remove any foreign body is to pour tepid water into the ear and let it float out. Do not poke in the ear because you could push the object farther inside.

NOSEBLEED

High altitude can cause bleeding from the nose. The victim should sit with his head forward to prevent blood from entering his throat. He should pinch just below the bridge of his nose, where the blood vessel passes across the cartilage, for 10 minutes. Repeat the pinching in 10-minute cycles until the bleeding ceases.

Pinch hard below bridge of nose

CRAMP

Cramp is a sudden, involuntary, and painful muscle spasm. It can be caused by strenuous exercise such as walking or swimming, or by the loss of excessive salt or fluid from the body through profuse sweating. To relieve a cramp in the back of the thigh, straighten the victim's knee by raising the leg. For a cramp in the front of the thigh, bend the knee. In each case, massage the muscle firmly with your fingers.

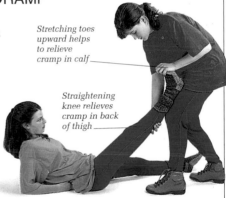

Stretching toes upward helps to relieve cramp in calf

Straightening knee relieves cramp in back of thigh

DIARRHEA AND VOMITING

Diarrhea and vomiting can cause severe dehydration. Ensure that you maintain your fluid level by sipping from a rehydration solution consisting of one teaspoon of salt, one tablespoon of sugar, and 1¾ pints (1 liter) of sterile water.

ANIMAL BITES

An animal bite carries the risk of bacterial infection, and a tetanus vaccination is a wise precaution for backpackers *(see page 17)*. Some animals infected with the rabies virus foam at the mouth or behave in a disoriented way, but others appear quite normal. For this reason, treatment should be sought after any animal bite.

Clean wound with plenty of cold water

1 An animal bite can puncture the skin and force bacteria deep into the underlying tissue. Treatment consists of pouring water over the wound for at least five minutes, as soon as possible after being bitten, to prevent infection.

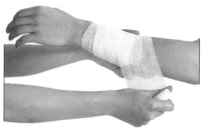

2 If the bite is deep and has caused bleeding, apply pressure with a gauze pad to stop the flow of blood. Keep the wound above the level of the heart and bandage the pad in place.

SNAKE BITES

A venomous snake bite may cause severe pain around the puncture marks, together with marked redness and swelling. Nausea and vomiting, disturbed vision, increased salivation, or sweating may result, and breathing may be labored or even cease altogether. Clean any snake bite thoroughly to reduce the risk of infection.

1 The victim is likely to be very frightened, so lay him down and tell him to keep calm. Panic increases the heartbeat, speeding up the rate at which the venom is circulated around the body. If you know that the snake was only mildly poisonous, wash the wound with soap and water. If you think the snake bite could be fatal, immediately apply direct pressure to the wound.

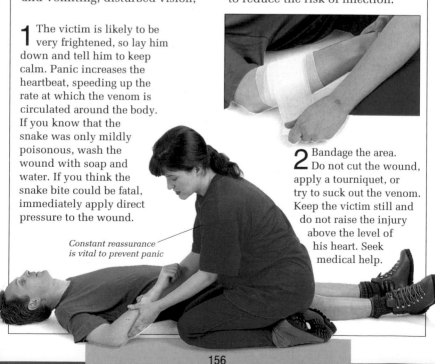

2 Bandage the area. Do not cut the wound, apply a tourniquet, or try to suck out the venom. Keep the victim still and do not raise the injury above the level of his heart. Seek medical help.

Constant reassurance is vital to prevent panic

INSECT STINGS

Bee, wasp, and hornet stings cause an initial sharp pain, followed by mild swelling and soreness. A bee often leaves its sting sac in the wound, and this should be scraped out with a knife blade. Wash the stung area with soap and water. Backpackers susceptible to anaphylactic shock after a sting should carry medication and instruct their group in its emergency use.

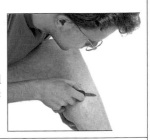

DANGEROUS DISEASES

Travel exposes the backpacker to many deadly diseases, caused by bacteria or viruses and transmitted in a variety of ways. Vaccinations and safe food and water protect the traveler against infection.

DANGEROUS DISEASES

Disease	Where found	How transmitted	Symptoms
AIDS/ HIV	Worldwide, especially Africa	Via blood, through sexual intercourse, hypodermic needles	None for many months
Cholera	Africa, Asia	Through extremely insanitary conditions	Nausea, diarrhea, vomiting, cramps, dehydration, shock
Hepatitis A (infectious hepatitis)	Worldwide	From the feces of infected people	Chills, fever, lethargy, loss of appetite, dark urine, pale feces
Poliomyelitis	Warm climates	From the feces of infected people	Chills, sore throat, loss of appetite. Later, headaches, paralysis
Typhoid	Mexico, Far East, Africa	From water contaminated with infected feces	Headache, abdominal pain, fever, delirium
Yellow fever	Central and South America	Via a mosquito bite	Headache, fever, limb pain, vomiting blood, constipation
Malaria	Far East, Africa, Central and South America	Via a mosquito bite	Fever, chills, shivering, headaches
Plague	Almost worldwide	Via bites from fleas from infected rodents	Fever, swollen lymph glands
Rabies	Almost worldwide	Via the saliva of infected animals	Fever, loss of appetite, hyperactivity, thirst, inability to drink, fright
Tetanus	Worldwide	Via spores entering wounds	Fever, muscle spasms, extreme fear, lockjaw, asphyxia

INDEX

ACKNOWLEDGMENTS

AUTHOR'S ACKNOWLEDGMENTS
As ever, the Dorling Kindersley editorial and design team deserve medals. Designer Colette Ho, for shoe-horning so much information into a very restricted space. Editor Francis Ritter, for shaping and coordinating the enormous mass of information from which this book was created, and for calmness, perspective, and down-to-earth common sense. Managing Editor Krystyna Mayer, and that will-o'-the-wisp Managing Art Editor Derek Coombes kept noses firmly applied to the grindstone, while maintaining a high standard of team morale.

PUBLISHER'S ACKNOWLEDGMENTS
Medical consultation:
Dorling Kindersley would like to acknowledge the help and advice of the British Red Cross and Paul Marcolini in presenting the first-aid techniques on pages 146–157 of this book.

Equipment and materials:
Grateful thanks to: Blacks Camping and Leisure; On Your Bike; Rohan Ltd.; Snow and Rock Sports Ltd.; and Y.H.A. Adventure Shops.

Key: t top, b (at beginning of entry) bottom, c center, l left, r right, a above,
b (at end of entry) below.

Artworks:
All artworks by Coral Mula except: John Bishop, small figures at top left of each section. Dorling Kindersley Cartography (James Mills-Hicks and John Plumer) 12–13c, 17t, 22c, 24c, 88cr, bra, br, 90b, 100b, 101, 136cl, 142c. Cressida Joyce 10, 11, 80, 88t, 97tl, tr, 111b. Doug Miller 32, 33t, 87t, c. John Woodcock 107tl, 132c, b, 135crb, br.

Photography:
All photography by Andy Crawford, Steve Gorton, and Tim Ridley except:
Ace Photo Agency 12bl, 15cl. Brathay Exploration Group 23tr. J. Allan Cash Photo Library 88tl, tr, cr, 104–105. Bruce Coleman 6tl, 13cr, 14tl, 15ca, tl, 67br, cb, 121tc, ca, cla, 127tr, 134bl, bc. Steven J. Cooling 144cl. Cotswold 36cl, 37tl. Peter Crump 68bl. James Davis Travel Photography 7tr. Europa Sport 36cr, 37cl. Ffotograff 25cr. Robert Harding 13tc, 14bl, 30–31, 43tr. Hutchison Library 6bl, 14cl, 28tr, 99br, 145tl, br. Image Bank 2, 8–9, 12cl, 64–65, 84br, tr, 99bra, 124–125. Frank Lane Picture Agency Ltd. 12cla, 67tl, 121cra, tr, 127tl, br. Magnum Photos Ltd. 15bl. Hugh McManners 23bla, 25tl, 28cl, bl, br, 29bl, 85tr, tl, 103tl, cl, cr, clb, bl, 109tr, 144bc. Nicholas Mellor 25br. Mountain Camera 4cl, 12br, 13tr, br, bl, 14cr, 21br, 24bl, 27br, cr, 71tl, tr, cl, 138bl. NHPA 17br, 67cla, 121c, cr, 121tl, cl. Oxford Scientific Films 67bl, bc, crb, cra, clb. Raleigh International 6cr, 13bc, 100cl. Royal Geographical Society 7br, 29c. South American Pictures 23bra. Stockfile 13tl. Tony Stone Images 15cr, 66br, 88cl, 127bl. Travel Ink Photo & Feature Library 23cl, bl, 138cl. Vango (Scotland) Ltd. 47tr, tl, cl, cr. Wild Country/Steve Bell (Himalayan Kingdoms)/Terra Nova Equipment Collection 47br. Wilderness Photographic Library 25tr. Zefa 12clb, 15tr, 145cl.

Picture research: Anna Lord.
Page make-up: Jonathan Harris.
Model maker: Peter Griffiths 106, 108–109c.